Love
& Life

Love
& Life

Dr. Laura Schlessinger, MFT

Humanix Books
www.humanixbooks.com

Humanix Books

Love & Life
Copyright © 2020 by Humanix Books
All rights reserved

Humanix Books, P.O. Box 20989, West Palm Beach, FL 33416, USA
www.humanixbooks.com | info@humanixbooks.com

Humanix Books is a division of Humanix Publishing, LLC. Its trademark, consisting of the words "Humanix," is registered in the Patent and Trademark Office and in other countries.

ISBN: 978-163006-125-8 (Hardcover)
ISBN: 978-163006-126-5 (E-book)

Printed in the United States of America
10 9 8 7 6 5 4 3 2 1

To all who practice:

"Good thoughts, good words, good deeds"
—Zoroastrian belief

and

To all who have trusted me to help them
be and do better in life and love

Contents

Preface

For 15 years I have written monthly columns for Newsmax, and I have appreciated Newsmax's loyalty and support. When it was suggested to me that a curated and edited selection of these columns would make a timely and useful book, I was touched. These are my thoughts on a range of subjects having to do with making the most out of life with relationships and purpose.

As I read the selections made by the publisher, I frankly was impressed by the thought that went into organizing and editing 15 years' worth of 12 columns per year. It was left to me to add the commentary surrounding each chapter and essay. A labor of love.

I have spent my life dedicated to helping people—admittedly with a blunt, frank, sometimes shocking style . . . but always with compassion toward those who are truly committed to morals, values, principles, and ethics but struggle with their childhood pain and nasty impediments to their well-being. After over four decades on radio, I am gratified on a daily basis that helping one caller may help many thousands of listeners.

Thank you to SiriusXM and Geoff Rich (business manager and friend) who continue to support my voice being heard, especially in a growing environment limiting the speech of those not popular with activist groups.

Read each section slowly, and think seriously about the messages. Converse about the concepts with those close to you . . . Let's try to perfect the world together.

PART ONE

LOVE & MARRIAGE

Joy does not come from unfettered, spontaneous revelry.
Joy comes from caring for someone who actually gives a damn.

The singularly most wonderful advice to ensure a quality life with another human being to whom you are committed was emailed to me from a gay man. He was playfully lamenting that straight folks are often quite negative about gay relationships, while their marital failure rate was so high. He thought the solution was quite simple: "CHOOSE WISELY, TREAT KINDLY."

Wow! Yup, I would say that most marital failures are based on not choosing wisely and not treating kindly.

Wake up every day, look over at your spouse, and plan what you will do to make your spouse happy that he or she is alive AND married to you!

CHAPTER ONE

Reality Check for Love

I will make it simple: Treat your spouse in the ways that would make YOU want to come home to YOU.

Five Secrets to a Satisfying Marriage

It started off as a routine call to my radio program. A husband and wife were on the line together wanting to know what they could do about their constant bickering and lack of intimacy. Their call was not about sex; they articulated their problem as not feeling close at all. They both work full-time, the husband then goes to school full-time in the evenings, and they have two children in day care.

Before I tell you what I said to them, let me tell you that I race sailboats with an experienced crew. We each have a task, and when each of us commits to fulfilling that task, we excel—to our mutual satisfaction.

My task is to drive the boat. I can't do that correctly unless the trimmers have the sails in their proper place; I also need my tactician to direct and the crew to alert me to wind puffs, swells, and other boats that can give me "disturbed air" or that I might collide with. My job is to keep my attention *inside* the boat in order to get the best performance out of the boat.

Similarly, families need to work as a *team*, with each member having areas of responsibility. When there is no one paying attention to making a house a home, making it a priority to properly raise the children, or nurturing a marriage, unhappiness, frustration, loneliness, and ultimately disconnection are almost a promise. The family capsizes.

To the couple I said, "There's just too much on your plate. This is a definite 'gave at the office' moment." The wife seemed relieved, probably feeling too overwhelmed and undernourished by her life, having little to no time with her children and husband, and not having the peace and joy of building a "home." Her husband got angry and began arguing with me. I sat there stunned. For me it was as though a tornado was clearly bearing down on us and he was denying that it could cause disaster.

I understand why he might be so entrenched in his rut. I understand why he and so many others have life backwards. Instead of working *for* family, they are working in spite of family. In an article published in *USA Today*, a study showed that "the costs of day care, preschools and nannies now consume so much of families' incomes that working parents are basing major decisions about their jobs and families on how much care they can afford. The costs are leading to wrenching choices . . . some are working more than they like so they can afford child care costs." The amazing aspect of this article was that having a mom or dad at home raising children was never indicated as a reasonable, respectable, or plausible choice!

The *Wall Street Journal* featured an article about power couples who, though they "have plenty of money to spend, have scant time to spend with each other." These are two of thousands of such presentations of acquisition, self-fulfillment, power, and status being more important than love, nurturance, raising children, and living a life where interpersonal obligations and family dynamics are tertiary (not even secondary).

One listener wrote me about this dilemma: "When I met my husband at 24, we were great together. Two years later we were married, had a baby, bought a home and I started a new career . . . all in one year. It was hectic. If this wasn't enough, after our daughter's birth, I had to continue with college courses and I nursed her for 15 months . . . which took time away from my husband." She admitted that there was too much on their plate, but they never pushed anything off.

After their second child, it just got worse, and they ended up divorcing. She ended her letter with, "I would hate for another marriage to end just because of pride and adults who think they have to take on the world . . . that we can do it all . . . wrong! It is really quite simple: Put your family first. Love one another. Communicate! Listen and stop trying to have everything in life."

Too true! Given these examples, here are five pointers on how to change your family life so that it is warmer, more satisfying, and more successful:

1. If you're unhappy, admit it! This is difficult for many people because they don't want to disappoint their spouse by not wanting to keep striving for more, more, more. Risk being open and vulnerable about your deepest thoughts about love, family, marriage, and life.

2. Listen to each other without argument and immediate judgment. When you truly love somebody, you need to show that not only with kisses and flowers, but also with tenderness when your spouse's soul is bared.

3. Write down lists of all the things each of you does and what you do together. Put them in an order of priority—be truthful.

4. Talk about these lists, your dreams in life, and your goals together.
5. Be willing to make sacrifices for the good of the marriage, children, and family.

There is a trade-off in life: When you're single you can do any darn thing you want, when you want. When you join lives in marriage with someone, the focus needs to be more outside the boat, with the satisfaction coming from joy, happiness, and appreciation, all of which, if you picked a good spouse, will result in your having more than you'd ever accumulate alone.

DR. LAURA SAYS:

Alice, a listener, makes the point poignantly:

Last year, we were shocked when my husband was diagnosed with leukemia. I was with him every day when he was in the hospital, and I stayed many nights to rub his feet or hold his hand. Sadly, he lost the battle several months later. Although, of course I wish I had more time with him, I have no regrets. You never know what the future holds, and I'm so thankful I spent my days dreaming up new ways to show him my love.

15 Minutes to Marital Peace

I'm often amazed at how a stern lecture from me on my radio program, a lecture that I thought was profound, will elicit little or no response, but a casual, whimsical aside will reverberate seemingly forever as folks incorporate the idea into their lives.

A woman caller once complained that her husband of more than two decades had an affair. What made this unusual was that her husband and the woman (who is also married) were coworkers, and they had had "15 minutes of sex" in his SUV every workday morning for 9 years!

The caller wanted to know if she could or should tell the woman's family, friends, and coworkers what she was doing—obviously to vent and gain some revenge.

I went into a commercial break after completing that call and kept thinking about the substance of the discussion I had with her. When I came back on the air, I said, almost absent-mindedly, "You know, considering how little intimacy there was for so long in that marriage, it might just be that the 15 minutes he spent with the coworker each morning kept him from leaving his marriage. Nine years is unfortunately longer than a lot of marriages. I wonder what would have happened in their marriage had they enjoyed each other for 15 minutes each morning?"

That was it. Not even 10 seconds of commentary. And the letters just keep coming, from local and national addresses.

From Thom: "I just finished listening to your show over the Internet. Your comment about the lady who was upset that her husband had been having an affair for nine years was right on. If my wife would do that, I would walk over hot coals every morning to bring her breakfast in bed and I would show up every day at lunchtime with a rose and a song. Heck, I would do all that if it was five minutes every week. But it's not. So far, it's been six years of void. My daughter will graduate in December, and so will I from a hollow marriage."

And on the more positive side, from Candace: "I am 23 years old and my husband is 26, and even at our young age it can be a challenge to keep things going in the bedroom."

She wrote that she had heard my comments, and "the next morning I woke up earlier than usual, looked at my husband and decided to initiate some 'play time.' Afterwards he said, 'What was that for?' I grabbed his face and kissed him and said, 'Because I love you.' He smiled and said, 'I love you too, and I think we should do this every morning and start the day off right!'"

And from Duane: "I listened to your suggestion that if the caller had similarly spent 15 minutes every morning, the problem would likely never have arisen. I think I'm the living proof. I've been married to my wife for almost 30 years, and she has made love to me almost every morning of all those years.

"I've had plenty of opportunities to stray—I won't deny that I'm attracted to other women—I'm attracted to all females! But I know I'm in the best situation that I could ever have in my life, and nothing would make me risk losing it."

DR. LAURA SAYS:

Just in case you are imagining that I am whitewashing affairs or blaming one person for the choice of another, you're wrong. What I am pointing out is that one 10-second thought—and 15 minutes of action—can make marriage a joy again.

True Love *Is* Conditional

"Unconditional love." It sounds so romantic, so accepting, so amazing. But in reality, it is such an unhealthy concept.

How can one unconditionally love a spouse who molests their children? How can one unconditionally love a child who murders innocent people? I realize I have selected extreme circumstances to make my point, but point made.

There ought to be no such concept as unconditional love. Yes, my friends, it is necessary to make judgments, to discern good from evil, sacred from profane, and right from wrong.

I was so impressed recently when the mother of an adult son called me on my radio program to tell me she was excommunicating him from her life. It seems he impregnated a recent girlfriend with no intention of marriage.

Mom called because she told her son in no uncertain terms that if he was going to go to the hospital the day of the birth, he was not to bring his current bimbo. He brought the bimbo. She was astonished at how unbelievably insensitive he was to do that to the mother of his child. She informed him that although he was her child, her flesh and blood, that his behavior was so totally unacceptable that she didn't wish to have contact with him.

Did it hurt her to do this? Of course it did. But in her mind it was necessary to maintain the dignity of her family. She took a stand. So few do.

There is the sad parade of mothers who hang onto their drugged-out, irresponsible, destructive children. Popular psychology has named these folks "enablers," in that they support the problem person as the person continues the problem behavior.

Enablers are not saints. They are largely people who hide their own inadequacies in total investment in the problem person. I don't believe for a moment that enablers are motivated by unconditional love. Rather, they are fulfilling their own emotionally unhealthy needs.

If you somehow force them to stop "enabling," they typically lapse into confusion and depression and generally feel lost. This is most evident when the problem person—on his or her own—decides to "clean up." It is typical for the enabler to do things to undermine any progress. Suddenly the unconditional love turns to anger and impatience.

The bottom line is this: Healthy love has conditions!

DR. LAURA SAYS:

In love and in life, and especially in marriage, it is necessary to make judgments, to discern good from evil, sacred from profane, and right from wrong and hold people accountable with consequences.

Romance, Not Sex, Defines Love

Cruising through news websites is something I do each morning. On one morning, one particular site announced the top 25 most romantic movies.

I was amazed at a number of the choices: An adult male dancer in a cheap resort "doing" a teenage girl . . . like they have a future. A woman having sex with her fiancé's younger brother. People who meet while on a European excursion and become intimate immediately, and so on.

When younger, I used to watch movies and get caught up in the mushy emotions. As an adult—and definitely as Dr. Laura—I watch movies on a much deeper level, and I'm not happy with the notion that as long as two people are swept up in fantasy and immediacy, it is just beautiful.

Maybe it's because I spend hours each day helping people extricate their hearts, minds, and collateral damage from their decisions to just go with the flow of erotic and romantic feelings.

I'm left trying to help them remedy the hurts done to others as well as themselves . . . and the "accidental" children who do not typically benefit from conception-on-the-run.

The African Queen was, to me, one of the most romantic movies of all time. Humphrey Bogart gives up being a surly, drunk, self-designated outcast for Katherine Hepburn, who gives up being an uptight, prissy, self-avowed spinster. They do this for a cause—using his little beat-up boat to sink a German warship.

Having that joint goal (well, she really had to work to get him out of his shell to be brave enough to rejoin the world), and having to deal with deadly elements on a six-foot power skiff, together, built something really romantic.

Those of you who are married and struggling with the economic elements or illnesses—whatever—should watch that movie together. Twice. I believe it will make you want to snuggle.

What brings people close together is not just sex. It is a joint goal—the attainment of which requires you both to become more. Sometimes that goal is survival; other times it is the birth of a child or a commitment to some effort in the world. Great sex is the prize. It is not the substance of true love.

DR. LAURA SAYS:

There can never be enough touching of skin or touching of heart.

Self-Centeredness Wrecks Marriages

It is so sad to me that so many people behave as though they are "sleeping with the enemy" when they're revving up for a dispute, argument, or all-out fight with the person they love.

When a caller starts describing his or her verbal altercation with a spouse, that caller seems to have such great clarity about what was wrong with the spouse's attitude or tone in the confrontation or what precipitated the spat.

When I ask the caller the simple question, "Yes, but why did you fight?" I usually get back only some further demonstration of how horrible or ultimately responsible the spouse was.

"But there is a fight only if two people engage in it," I reply. "You are explaining your spouse's supposed motivation, but what was yours?" I get silence back. Rarely, I then get some admission of shared responsibility.

The main issue for me is this: If your spouse is really mean, dangerous, or destructive, then you should be outta there! More often than not, the caller admits that the spouse is really a good person.

Okay, so let's get to what really causes you to start or join a fight: self-centeredness. Those are some fightin' words!

Think about it. When you are tired or frustrated, it is natural to be short-tempered and self-involved. That's the time to say, "Oops, sorry. I'm just so frazzled. I didn't mean to take it out on you."

Why don't we do that? It sounds so rational. The trouble is, when we're tired or frustrated, it is tough to be rational. But it is absolutely necessary to explain and apologize as well as to work harder to stop yourself from getting into that bad place in the first place.

Some people just get so invested in being perfect in their work, housekeeping, or childcare. They start to view their commitment to making their spouse happy as an intruding inconvenience instead of a blessing. They get short-tempered and rude with the one they're supposed to adore instead of turning to their partner for support.

Another aspect of self-centeredness in such fighting comes from having to be "right." When couples fight, each is trying to prove to be in the right. Why? Because the underlying fear is that if the person is wrong, he or she won't be loved. That obviously stems from childhood dynamics with parents who are excessively punitive or who were stingy with love, affection, attention, and approval.

Of course, arguing all the time in order to be loved is counterintuitive as well as counterproductive, but it goes on and on and on.

Ultimately, there comes to bear the "sleeping with the enemy" attitude, born of early childhood experiences with warring parents or divorced parents who keep attacking each other, trying to win the children to their side, and never letting go of grievances and evil manipulations.

Want to really be assured of everlasting love? Try to prove your spouse right. You can do that in one of two special ways. First, simply own up to the fact that your spouse has a point and say it: "Honey, you're right. I could have said that differently and taken your feelings more into account. I'm sorry."

Not only will your spouse melt, but you will find yourself getting immediate love and affection.

Another way of assuring everlasting love, and proving your spouse right, is to sit together when you're having a difficult and painful dispute and say, "Look, all I can see is my point of view. All I care about right now is being the one who is right. Let's try something. Each of us gets a turn to express why we are upset, angry, or hurt without the other commenting at all even if we don't see it that way. At the end of each explanation, the other person must—like a defense attorney in a trial—give the best possible argument for the other's point of view."

When we have to look at it from the other's point of view, we immediately get out of self-centeredness and get into compassion mode—and nothing binds people together more than feeling understood and feeling compassion for our feelings. It makes us more likely to stop exaggerating and attacking to protect, and more likely to become more reasonable and giving toward our spouse.

DR. LAURA SAYS:

Once you choose wisely, make sure not to have knee-jerk emotional reactions, but to give the benefit of the doubt.

In Marriage, Spouse Comes Before Parents

On my radio show, a call came in from a frustrated wife. She married a man whose father had disappeared soon after her husband was born. His mother then drop-kicked him to grandma's house so she could take off, too. He was raised by his grandparents, who loved and cared for him his whole childhood.

Now that he is a married man in his thirties, he can count on one-and-a-half hands how often he has been contacted by his mother.

My caller described the situation: "We were planning our vacation. My husband said he made a simple mistake by telling his company that he would take a certain week off, not realizing that our special needs child still had school." The wife was annoyed but tried to make the best out of it by suggesting, to his agreement, that after dropping their daughter off at school, they would take romantic, interesting day trips and then pick their daughter up after school. They had five wonderful days planned, and she was content that they could focus on each other.

Then he called from work to tell her that his so-called mother contacted him and wanted to visit the same week the vacation was planned.

He told his wife that he invited his so-called mother to stay at their home!

He didn't talk to his wife about it—he just announced it to her, and she was fit to be tied.

I suggested that when she hangs up from our conversation, she call her husband and say, "No. This is our special time, and I don't think it is reasonable for you to have your non-mother in our home, especially without discussing it with me, and having our vacation plans put aside. The answer is no. No, I will not have her in my home. You can go to a motel with her if you want to spend time with her."

Adults who have been betrayed, abused, abandoned, and even tortured by their parents often still have a fantasy that mommy or daddy will come back to love them. While I explained that aspect to the caller, I urged her not to let him abandon his responsibilities to her, as his mother had done to him.

The caller got back to me on the air again and said that after she gave him all this information, he very emotionally said, "Okay, I will tell her to stay home." He was angry that his fantasy would not have an opportunity. Sad—really sad.

DR. LAURA SAYS:

Some folks too often forget they made their vows to their spouse—not their parents. This confusion is a prime source of discord in marriages.

REFLECTIONS

Over the years I have talked to people who threw away perfectly good marriages and those who brought marriage back from the brink.

Vilma wrote concerning the former:

I left my husband of 26 years four years ago. I convinced myself that he was at fault for everything wrong with our marriage. I spoke badly about him to friends and family and convinced them that he was the cause of my terribly miserable life. After I left, he refused to ever speak to me again. When our divorce was final I got alimony, but he got happiness. I was not there ridiculing his every move. I was not there complaining that he was not this or that. I now realize that I behaved like a rotten, spoiled brat.

I wrote him a letter of apology, because he deserved it. I hoped and prayed that he would forgive me. He is now remarried, hopefully to a woman who appreciates all the same things he did for me. He probably wakes up every day with a smile. I hope she listens to you and takes your advice. I found you too late. It doesn't matter that I thought I was a good wife and that I did a lot of kind, loving things for him, because I tore them all down and crushed his heart and soul.

Ladies, please take care of your husband and listen to Dr. Laura or you will be left with a broken heart that he had nothing to do with. I did this all to myself and I want others to learn from my mistakes. No one deserves to be the recipient of the behavior I inflicted on my husband.

That is, unfortunately, a frequent lament.

As for the latter, bringing a marriage back from the brink, an email from Jerry, a former Navy fighter pilot struggling with PTSD from combat experience, wrote:

I dropped a lot of bombs on targets in the Middle East and I know a lot of people died as a result. Although I tried to have a clear conscience, knowing that most of the victims were the enemy, they were still human with families who loved them.

I really needed to open up to my wife but I thought she would think I was weak. The turning point for me was finding your radio program on SiriusXM. I started to listen to you every day on my commute. I learned so much from you on marriage that I finally worked up the courage to open up to my wife. I let it all out. I cried like a baby telling her about my experiences and the struggles that were haunting me. She held me tight and kept telling me that she was here for me and to just let it all out. Once I stopped crying, it felt like a huge burden was lifted from my soul. I feel a thousand percent better and know my relationship with my wife went to a very high level that night. I know she will always be there for me as I continue to heal. Thanks for giving me the strength to open up to my prized bride.

Your spouse is the one person in the world you must be able to trust with your deepest self.

CHAPTER TWO

For Women Only

Security in a marriage comes from you fulfilling the vows you made to love, honor, and cherish. Again: love, honor, and cherish. Okay, now decide on how you are going to speak to your spouse.

Be a Girlfriend to Your Husband

Many women I talk to suffer from feminist brainwashing that is pervasive today. With so much unhappiness in marriages today, I often wonder how I can reach more women to offer them a different perspective—one that might help them survive the challenges of marriage. My goal is to help women become who their husbands would love to come home to. As it often happens, a young woman, a millennial, called my radio show and these very issues came up.

She told me that she and her husband dated for four years before they got married. After getting married, she stayed back in their hometown to finish up her teaching contract while he began a new job in the city. After about six months she was able to move in with him in the city. She told me they fought, but other than that she thought everything was all right.

That was the first warning flag—thinking everything was all right when there was fighting going on. Fighting is *not* a normal part of a good marriage. A substantial amount of fighting shows an unhealthy relationship.

She had recently returned from a work-related trip when her husband told her that while he loved her, he was not very happy. He told her that he thought he could handle her personality, but now he was not so sure. He had lost his patience. He told her she doesn't think for herself as much as she should. Naturally, my first question to her was, does your husband want to leave you? She said, "He hasn't said he's going to, but he wants us to take it one day at a time...."

I learned that this young wife wanted to figure out how to fix her marriage. She also wanted to improve aspects of her personality for her own sake. I had a plan for her: Don't say anything to your husband that isn't sweet. No bitching, no complaining, no whining.

Impossible, no! Necessary, yes! Let me explain.

Whining and complaining are not how you should treat your man—especially after you are married. Marriage turns a man from "patient boyfriend" to "husband who doesn't want this crap." He doesn't want to see the rest of his life like this. A man will always want to be with a "girlfriend." A man will fool around on his wife because the wife has turned into an ogre, and now he wants that girlfriend again! Girlfriends don't bitch, fight, criticize, or nag. That's because girlfriends know their boyfriends will leave.

I had to break the news to her that her husband was, in fact, preparing to leave her, and that she better act fast if she wanted to save her marriage. In addition to stopping the whining, I told her to stop texting. Seems impossible, but also necessary! Actually talk to him in the real world. I told her to call her husband once a day to say something naughty, or adorable, or both. How about, "Honey, this is your girlfriend calling. Don't let your wife know!"

He's sure to laugh. Texting isn't good for most people anyway, but especially for this millennial, because she has been tormented by trying to analyze what people are trying to say in a text. No text, no torment, because she will only have real conversations.

And here's what I say to all women: Follow my plan and you're going to be happier. We need to do things that bring peace and joy. Some people use music; some people use prayer; some people use exercise. Doing good deeds, being sweet, that's how we begin to feel good, and if you treat your husband sweetly, *you* are going to be happier than you've been, because you haven't been happy if your marriage isn't good.

DR. LAURA SAYS:

In some cases—not all—it's my experience that if women would just take a moment and reflect on what it is they're saying, how they're reacting, they would give more thought to the words they're using. And please, let's stop texting for a bit and have a real, honest-to-goodness conversation. Your spouse will thank you.

Mind Your Man

I had a meltdown, once, on my radio program. This had never happened before, but I followed it up with what I thought was right: I apologized immediately to the caller and the listeners.

Here's what set me off: During a single program, I had three women with the same unbelievably selfish attitude toward their children. The first woman dated a man who admitted to enjoying sex with either men or women but was making a choice to sticking with women after meeting her. Fully knowing that he continued to "communicate" with men, she married him, had two children, and is now furious that he is back with men again. I asked her how she could marry a man with confused sexuality and bring children in this situation.

A second caller met a guy on the Internet and had unprotected sex almost immediately. She got pregnant and married him, and now she is furious that he is so immature. Really?

A third woman—the one who cocked my trigger—was married to a guy 10 years older who retired at 56 and now sits at home with the 10-year-old daughter when she is home from school. The wife is furious that he won't do housework.

Each of them wanted to dump the husbands, in spite of having children who would be damaged not just by divorce, but also by terrible choices and actions of the parents as they "move on."

The third female caller just wouldn't absorb my exhorting her to make the best of the situation for the benefit of her children. She didn't even touch that concept with the tip of her finger, much less discuss how that might happen. Instead, she repetitively went into the same mode of the other two: "But what about my needs?" After I tried to reach her several times, she just started to rant about her needs and happiness, etc., and when I couldn't get a word in, I finally actually yelled, "Shut the hell up!"

I immediately apologized for being rude. I calmly repeated that she owed her children a peaceful, stable life with two parents who love them in spite of the two parents not particularly being loving to each other. Sometimes friendship looks better than the cycle of disappointments, frustrations, and annoyances.

It is very clear to me that the post–baby boomer generation and their offspring have morphed generally into selfish and irresponsible beings. Too many of my callers respond to my questions about the dating phase of coming to know each other and their respective families with stories of quickie sex and marriage after Internet meetings, or almost immediate sex and pregnancy, or ignorance about the temporary emotional high of infatuation, or a desperate attempt to run away from themselves by marrying a problem person to fix that person or respond to the first person who shows attention.

All of this is coming to mean to me that "there ought to be a law" that people cannot marry unless they finish nine months (like the gestation of a human baby) of premarital counseling where a trained professional has them examine themselves and explore all the important issues of marriage: money, extended family, housekeeping, children and childcare, finances, geography, free time, closeness to family of origin, and so forth.

After sleeping on my outburst, I think it did serve a positive function. Just about all of us have to deal with selfish people in our lives. I can't even count how many times I have told folks to hold those people accountable and call them on their actions. It is called communication, and it is necessary for human relationships and an individual holding on to sanity versus taking continued insensitivity or abuse. Good people tend to be incredibly wishy-washy about standing up and saying out loud that there is an elephant in the room. I urge others to stand up for what is right, fair, and kind.

It is truly upsetting that so many women get their children into untenable situations and then destroy their families in the search for "their needs always being met." The heck with the needs of their children or their spouse.

People can create lovely environments even when they "don't feel the love" they fantasize about because they are moral adults who put the well-being of their children and the potential growth of their marriage above their selfishness.

DR. LAURA SAYS:

A good woman can bring the best out of her man when she appreciates his needs. Unfortunately, feminism has undermined this beautiful truth.

Home Should Represent Fulfillment

Mother's Day is a source of stress for many women who are sole providers and can't be hands-on moms or feel intimidated by a culture that doesn't value hands-on moms.

The feminist movement has attempted to reconfigure the traditional family under the guise that gender isn't significant for women, child-rearing, and the quality of marriage. As a result, women feel guilty for yearning to raise their own children.

Women's and parenting magazines declare that the most important thing a woman can do is make herself happy (through work), or maintain power (her own bank account), and of course, make sure that one of the representatives of the evil empire (a man/husband) does not oppress her.

Guess what? Women these days are less happy (missing the joys of developing and loving children) and more frenzied (trying to be and do everything).

Many moms tell me they get bored at home. Here's a letter I received from one such woman and how she resolved her malaise:

Hello Dr. Laura,
A year ago, my mother gave me your book, *In Praise of Stay-at-Home Moms*, for Mother's Day. I shared a lot of what I read with my husband. By the end of the book, there was no doubt that my place was at home with our son.

We figured out a budget and I put in my two-weeks' notice. It's the best thing I have ever done. I get to be my son's mom and my husband's girlfriend.

At first, my son and I would go on play dates and picnics and have so much fun. Recently, however, I've been feeling bored.

One night I was watching the movie *Julie & Julia*, and it clicked. I could find new things to do with my son and blog about it. Even if no one ever reads it now, my son can read it when he's older.

I started making a list of all the things we could do. Of course, since we are a single-income family, I have to keep it cheap. The next day I started my blog. A month later, I have 18 followers. I never considered myself a writer, but people are reading it, and leaving lovely comments.

Thank you so much for everything you do, Dr. Laura.

I tell women that at home they truly have time to grow spiritually, intellectually, and physically. They also lose much of their feminist-trained hostility toward their husbands and gain back the blessing of their sexuality. Once I'm done with them, they develop a deeper appreciation for how they are singularly responsible for the attitude and atmosphere of their home.

DR. LAURA SAYS:

Nick, a listener, wrote in:

My wife and I have been married for eight years and have three boys. We worked opposite shifts but she said she didn't want to work anymore. I was nervous about not having the extra income, but once I heard YOU, you made it all clear to me that it wasn't

> about the money. It was about having a better relationship with
> my wife and family. Since she's been home taking care of the kids
> and me, we've been closer to one another than ever and the kids'
> attitudes have changed dramatically. Dr. Laura, you have changed
> my family's life for the better.

I thought you would like to hear it from the husband's point
of view!

Lack of Morality in Relationships Is No Laughing Matter

The story I am about to tell you may sound implausible, but I
assure you it is not only completely true but representative of
what is going on in America today with respect to "relationships."

Ever since the collective attitude turned away from any rules
of propriety, modesty, morality, and frankly, good sense, stories
like this have become everyday occurrences.

Here goes: A caller to my radio show reports that she has been
dating and having sexual relations with a man who is shacking up
with another woman. Our caller, in her early forties, doesn't see
that she is doing anything wrong by being with another woman's
man because, after all, they are not married. So much for feminist
sisterhood!

Not only does she not see this as wrong or foolish, but she has
expectations of how he is supposed to treat her.

Excuse me? Expectations? Based on what? An occasional roll
in the hay?

When I asked her how she possibly could expect anything
other than an occasional "booty call," she replied that he owes her
because she is sexually available to him.

"I love him," she said.

I sarcastically responded with, "Certainly you love him. He has all the qualities of a decent, loving, faithful man."

And then I laughed. I laughed really hard.

So here we are with women liberated from their shackles of the double standard (sarcasm very intended) performing the services of prostitutes without the good financial sense to collect the cash.

As though to corroborate my assessment of this fellow as less than noble, she continued, "And it turns out that there are two other women involved."

I couldn't help but laugh again. But this is not a laughing matter.

The motivation behind everything from marital commitments to the double standard was to elevate and protect the sanctity of a woman's body, soul, psyche, and value as well as to protect potential offspring. Many women have voluntarily surrendered this good stuff so they can be "unpaid whores."

The emotional needs of women have not changed. Women want to be wanted, loved, protected, provided for, and cherished. There has been no DNA mutation that has unraveled this hard wiring of a woman's psychological needs.

But today, there are women who have serious emotional problems from early family experiences who may find it uncomfortable to form a healthy relationship with a really substantial man. Many of them are products of women like my caller who don't bother to build a sturdy nest before making babies. That chaos leads to fears, unfamiliarity, and cynicism about love and commitment.

I am not laughing any more.

DR. LAURA SAYS:

Next time you are having to make a decision about what to do or say, think "What would a LADY do."

REFLECTIONS

A young woman of 22 called my program to express discomfort about being sexually active with her boyfriend of a little over a year. She explained that listening to my program made her think more about the concept of "being a lady" and making sex something special through the loving commitment of marriage. She wasn't sure how to phrase this to him. I suggested: "Sweetie, I care about you very much, but the next time I have sex it will be with my husband."

She called back a month later and said, "He was appreciative that I would be open. He said he was happy to treat me like the lady I was and would wait as long as I wanted to get married and then have sex!" Sublime.

CHAPTER THREE

Husbands & Wives

Ask not what your marriage can do for you . . . ask only what you can do for your marriage. If you choose wisely, it will be reciprocated!

Make Time to Be Sweet and Loving

There is a very old, silly joke that is brilliant in its simplicity. A patient complains to the doctor that every time he hits his hand on the table it hurts. The patient is anxious for a cure. The doctor says, simply, "Well, just stop hitting your hand on the table."

I get many calls from listeners to my radio program about how unhappy, frustrated, and demoralized they are with some aspect of their lives. They explain in great detail what is causing their suffering, but the truth is, it is never anything from within that list.

One woman complained that her husband is distant from her. I wondered aloud if he were afraid of disappointment or confrontation if he approached her with his feelings or needs. Fortunately, this caller was open to exploring her own contribution to the situation.

I asked her if she was as sweet, silly, and loving as she was earlier on in their relationship. She admitted she was not and immediately, though, jumped into excuses of time, children, work, finances, and on and on. I stopped her and suggested that should she continue to give all these issues priority over sweet, silly, and loving, the path of their marriage might disappear over the horizon.

She called back a few weeks later and was ecstatic that they were having such a good time together and that things between them were so warm. I asked her what changed. She answered, "I just turned the sweet, silly, and loving back on. And it is amazing how quickly everything seemed to turn around. I don't know if it is my husband or men in general, but he gave into the new inter-action with me without recriminations. He just seemed to get with things immediately. It has been wonderful."

Just sweet, silly and loving. How much time does that take? It is like powdered sugar sprinkled gently across the landscape of a relationship. No big debates, conversations, or confrontations.

Valentine's Day is only once a year, but the concept (minus the commercialism) of taking a day to refocus priorities in your love relationship is a necessary one. When I first began an earlier Valentine's Day radio program, I did not go on and on with lists of to-dos and not-to-dos. I began simply with: "A great relation-ship requires two main choices. The first is that you choose wisely. The second is that you treat kindly."

"We just grew apart" is nonsense. People do not grow apart. That is not accurate at all. People let go. People get self-absorbed and ignore their moral and loving responsibility to make a prior-ity out of their spouse's feelings and needs. People get petty when they are inconvenienced, as in complaints about socks left on the floor. "Well," I said to one complaining caller, "it means you are not alone."

It is also true that very often our life choices do not necessar-ily contribute to the well-being of our own psyches, much less the well-being of our family and marriage. Here is an example of how choices are always open to change—if you have the guts.

Late in January I received an email from a listener:

> I am the product of the women's lib movement. My parents encouraged me to pursue my education as high as possible. The end result was my delivering my first baby at the end of my medical residency. I was expected to pursue an intensive fellowship and continue research.
>
> It wasn't until I was pregnant that the grave implications of my career path and decision to be a mother hit me. I wept, realizing that I had a few months to find another woman to raise my child. I felt trapped. My husband, also a doctor, had a similar epiphany. I turned down the fellowship that I had worked so hard for, to the dismay of my colleagues, who all thought a nanny was a great solution.
>
> When I announced my decision to leave and be a stay-at-home mom, I came under heavy criticism about my wasted talent and education. My husband stood by my side. You encouraged me through your program. It is now 16 years later and we have two boys and a girl. I am able to work on a contingent basis for local doctors, because even though my children are old enough to be left alone, they need me even more now, as does my husband.

Here it comes!

> Our marriage thrived after I stopped working too. I had time to be my husband's girlfriend and there were no longer arguments over whose career was more important. I have not once looked back and thought about who I could have been. I look to the future with peace.

DR. LAURA SAYS:

One of my listeners, Millie, wrote to me about the result of treating her man with affection, attention, admiration, and some good lovin': "My husband tells me I'm beautiful on my grubbiest days, because that's what his heart sees."

Happy Spouse in the House

I recently received an email from a male listener who signed off as "a happy husband." Smiling, I began to read the text of his letter immediately, imagining that he was going to be telling me all the wondrous things his wonderful wife does for him. I was wrong . . . happily so. Here's his letter:

> I'm a real man who's lucky to have a beautiful and smart woman as my wife of 13 years. These are the things I do to keep us both happy:
>
> 1. Ask myself every morning: What will I do today to make her appreciate marrying me?
> 2. Pay for a housekeeper. I've had housekeepers since I was in graduate school. I can afford one, so I hired one for our family. My wife shows me her appreciation (wink, wink) for this one big time!
> 3. Clean up and help around the house. Our agreement is that she cooks and I clean up. Works for me.
> 4. Cook a meal sometimes or do something that she usually does. It's the thought that counts, even if the meal isn't as delectable as one she'd make.

5. Write little notes and do little things for her. Sometimes I leave a note several pages ahead in whatever she's reading.

6. Appreciate her wanting to keep herself looking good when she goes to the hair or nail salon. Don't complain about the outrageous bills. Appreciate the beauty and budget it in every month or so.

7. Keep her vehicle clean and running well.

8. Be open and honest, and not afraid to ask for what I want or say what I like.

9. Keep myself healthy and clean and in shape, so I'll remain attractive to her.

10. Occasionally take a couples cruise or go to a couples resort.

11. Send flowers to her mother on my wife's birthday . . . thanking her mom for bringing my wife into this world.

It's all of these things and more rolled up together that make me . . . a happy husband.

I was thrilled that this man realized that the way to be a happy husband was to ask not what his wife can do for him, but ask what he can do for his wife, family, and marriage.

Often when I point this truth out to folks, they get defensive and start complaining about what their spouses (chosen by them, remember?) do or don't do, or they point out that things must be reciprocal. I speak to too many women in particular on my radio program whose husbands are leaving and divorcing them. Nine out of ten times they finally admit that they stopped being his girlfriend once married; and even worse, either they became a critical nagging mother, or they just neglected their husbands because they were overinvolved with the children and/or their relatives.

Happy husbands don't typically fool around, nor do they leave. And as I have pointed out in my book *The Proper Care and Feeding of Husbands,* men are not complicated. If a man has his woman's respect, affection, and attention, neither wild horses nor a naked coworker could take him away from her . . . assuming he is not a sociopath, narcissist, or addict, of course; those men are the exception and not the rule, even though angry women love to diagnose any man who doesn't do what they want as a narcissist.

I have gotten into a lot of trouble with feminists who refuse to have any woman take any responsibility for a starved husband's affair. Of course he is breaking his vows. However, the vows are to love, honor, and cherish. So when a woman ceases to live up to those vows and emotionally and physically starves her husband for years, should she not assume some responsibility for his desperation? I think yes.

DR. LAURA SAYS:

How wonderful it is when men take loving responsibility for the proper care and feeding of their wives.

Get Intimate!

It's a cliché I hear too often: Husbands complain that wives are not interested in sex anymore.

When a woman calls my radio program with this issue, I ask a number of questions to determine the foundation of the problem: "Did you ever enjoy sex?" "Did you ever enjoy sex with your husband?" "Is he a good lover?" I ask her if she is overstressed, tired, angry at him for something, frustrated with daily life, having medical issues? Mostly I get back that she is tired at the end of the day and feels as though she's given enough of herself and resents his "need" for sex.

On one such husband-wife call, the husband started by saying that he tried everything to entice her, but she shut him down most of the time and it just hurts. He was frustrated because he didn't know what to do to return to intimacy. She responded by saying she didn't need sex to feel intimate ... talking and cuddling did it for her. Here's what I made sure she understood:

1. She was right—for women, talking and cuddling is intimacy. For men, sexual contact is intimacy.
2. If she didn't want to accept and honor the differences between men and women, she should consider terminating the marriage and marrying another woman, as they would be on the same page.

The husband agreed with my assessment: "Yes, that's right—we measure intimacy differently."

I explained to the wife that for men, the union of bodies is perceived as love. That means that every time she shuts him down, he assumes waning love is the reason.

After this foundation, I began to focus on the act itself. "How do you feel after an orgasm?" I asked.

She replied, "Great."

"Well," I said, "why in the world would you cut yourself off from feeling really, really good after a long day of responsibilities?"

She answered, "Well, I am just not feeling interested."

"Great," I countered, happy to have found a place for us to start.

My next question: "The times you went ahead with the program in spite of not feeling like it, did you end up with a massive smile on your face?"

"Yes," she said.

"Well then," I pointed out, "it seems that we can get you all the great post-sex feelings you enjoy by figuring out how to get past that initial 'blah' feeling. How about you have a mantra for when he starts? Make this your mantra: 'In a few moments I am going to feel amazingly wonderful.'"

I had her repeat this mantra several times right then and there.

I then illustrated my pitch by way of an example from the movie *Gone with the Wind*. I told her: "Rhett Butler was married to a difficult woman, Scarlett, who was in love with a weenie of a guy instead of the marvelous alpha male her husband was. One night, drunk, he lifted her off her feet and carried her up a huge flight of stairs and rocked her world—and she fought him all the way up the stairs. However, in the morning she was all smiles . . . until he came into her bedroom and apologized for taking her against her will because he was drunk and frustrated that she wouldn't love him. She is such a jerk that she doesn't tell him the truth . . . and he leaves her."

The wife gasped. I guess she got my message—being rejected doesn't work forever as a technique for keeping a man.

I have asked other wives who were resentful of their husband's desire for them whether they suggested he visit prostitutes, get a girlfriend, view porn, or leave them. They always say, "None of the above." I tell them that one of those is going to happen because their husband agreed to be married—not join some cult of abstinence.

The wife was happy with the idea I presented: that she should never again think of sex as giving him what he wants. Instead, she should see him as responsible for her greatest pleasure. Ultimately, she realized that sexual pleasure was hers to have and he was the means to that end.

DR. LAURA SAYS:

Never let annoyances, irritations, frustrations, pettiness, or anything else get in the way of a perfectly good orgasm with your man!

The Laundry Can Wait

Many women whine about how their spouse doesn't do nice things for them—like remember birthdays and anniversaries, spend time with them, come home early, and on and on.

I had a "fun" conversation with one wife who was furious that her husband complained about the piles of laundry that never seem to go away.

I asked whether her husband feels affection and appreciation from her. She answered that he probably would say that he feels neglected and that the romance had gone out of the relationship. I suggested that if she became his "girlfriend" and complimented, flirted, and seduced him, he would never notice the laundry.

Men who are emotionally and physically satisfied by their wives tend not to be nitpicky about small things because they are happy. Unhappy men tend to nitpick about details as a way of venting their pain.

A few days later, I received this email:

I was listening to a podcast a few days ago about a woman whose husband was upset because she had piles of laundry to do. You told her to take better care of him and he wouldn't be as negative.

It just so happens that it was laundry day at our house. I had piles of laundry all over the basement and laundry room. In the middle of my day before it was finished, my daughter's nap time came around. She went to sleep. I looked at the piles of laundry and thought, "Should I fold all of this or text my husband to come home for a little fun?"

So I texted my husband and needless to say, I didn't have time to get the laundry folded. When my husband left, our daughter woke up. Then dinner time rolled around. The laundry still didn't get done.

After dinner a man showed up at our house to give us an estimate for installing sprinklers. I was washing dishes when he came into the house with my husband and they headed straight for the basement . . . GASP!!! I was so embarrassed. They needed to inspect the pipes in the laundry room. Ugh! I was trying to figure out something cute or funny I could say about the giant mess.

I was sure my husband would bring it up. But not a word!

Later that night I said something about how I was mortified when I saw them go downstairs to that mess. My husband said, "Everybody has laundry." And then he gave me a kiss.

YOU WERE RIGHT! And I thought it was a funny coincidence that it happened on the exact day I listened to the call. Thanks, Beth.

DR. LAURA SAYS:

When spouses treat each other lovingly, playfully, and thoughtfully, there rarely is any nitpicking about laundry or anything else.

REFLECTIONS

In marriage, when there is some difference in opinion (and there will be!)—ferocious or mild—compromise with the person who feels the most passionate about his or her opinion. Your turn will come for a return of that favor.

Also, when there is a problem, don't think first about how to get your way and how angry you're going to be if you don't get it. A better way to solve the problem is to come up with some plan for making the other person feel better about the problem.

In fact, when you mess up—intentionally or not—remember the following four *R*'s; they are the lifeblood of a marriage:

1. **Remorse.** Truly feeling regret in your heart and soul for the damage and hurt you caused—without excuses and without blaming others for causing your actions.
2. **Responsibility.** Admitting to your actions and motives, and being willing to accept consequences and endure the other's pain and disdain until issues are resolved and feelings healed.
3. **Repair.** Doing whatever you can, directly or indirectly, to repair the damage. Sometimes this is not possible—but perhaps you can find a meaningful way to pay back the universe by lecturing others about drinking and driving or drug use or abuse.
4. **Repetition.** AKA not *repeating* the same mistake. Making the kinds of changes in your decisions, actions, and reactions that will definitely stand in the way of any repeat of the unpleasant actions.

These steps are necessary because people need to regain trust in you, and without your demonstration of effort, your words will seem empty.

A good marriage is both delicate and durable. Forgiveness will likely come once you've earned it.

It takes your willingness to treat your spouse as if you loved him or her with your last breath—no matter how you feel at any one moment. You need to think hard every day about how you can make your spouse's life worth living, and be the kind of person you would want to love, hug, come home to, and sacrifice for.

CHAPTER FOUR

Stay or Go?

The vast majority of divorced folks realize some five years later that they made a mistake. All-or-none thinking or only seeing the world through your emotional reactions may cause you to give up on someone whom you could be happy with again. Remember, a cup half empty exists to be refilled.

Accepting Marital Reality

I received a letter from a woman who describes a frequent bind that people either create or discover:

> My husband is a pastor and we are well known among certain groups of people. I would like to hear your ideas or suggestions on what a wife is to do when her husband says he cannot give her the love and affection she craves.

She goes on in the third person:

> If there was a deep hurt by the wife that has not been forgotten or completely forgiven by the husband, then is the marriage a hopeless case?
>
> The hurt is brought up at times when she mentions her needs, which has always been a major problem in this

marriage. What should a wife do when she has done all she can and there is not the option of a way out? What are your suggestions of coping with this situation?

From the tone of this letter, it would seem likely that the writer had sought and/or received attention and affection from someone outside the marriage.

While it is usually more difficult for a husband to accept that occurrence than most wives, being a Christian pastor would seem to ensure a higher degree of compassionate forgiveness.

But her statement that his not meeting her needs for affection and attention "has always been a major problem in this marriage" leads me to wonder if he isn't just constantly "using" his hurt feelings to justify what was already a problem for him: giving love.

It is not unusual for someone to be more comfortable with the adoration of others from afar, like a minister's flock, than with the more intimate obligations of a personal relationship.

This pastor might secretly be gay, or fearful of vulnerability because of childhood familial relationships, or simply narcissistic.

If he is unwilling to budge, his wife has only three choices:

- **Leave.** While she says it is not an option, of course it is—although divorce would mean sharing children, living on an uncomfortable budget, losing social standing, dealing with being alone, and so forth.
- **Stay and suffer.** The most typical option, as people do not wish to accept the reality of the circumstance because they want the happy ending—and I can't blame anyone for that! However, struggling against the unmovable is only masochistic and unproductive.
- **Stay and stop fighting reality.** She would accept that she lives in an emotional non-marriage, but that the family structure

and social ties and activities become the paramount personal issue, and the need for acceptance and approval becomes sublimated into hobbies, children, charity, and community activities.

This perspective is important not only in certain marriages, but in families and at work. Shannon, married with one small child, called my radio program recently to complain bitterly and painfully about her father hurting her emotionally.

He left the family early in her childhood and, in his alcoholic mindset, gives her very little in the way of father-daughter attention, love, and affection.

As she went on and on during the call, escalating to crying, I tried to stop her dead in her emotional tracks.

"Shannon, you are a grown woman. You are old enough to start looking at reality and accepting it. Your father is a bit of a drunk and a jerk. Instead of realizing and accepting that you can't get passion-fruit iced tea from a milk container, you keep squeezing that container and suffering over the lack of tea."

She came back with, "But I need to be filled up with father love. Isn't there anything I can do?"

That's when I reminded her of her husband and child.

"How do you think it feels to your husband that he can't fill you up?"

Shannon said, "Bad, probably. I didn't think of that."

"We each need to be filled up with loving, kind attention from the special people in our lives. When water can't get out one way, it goes another route. Water doesn't have a brain; you do. You aren't getting what you need from your father, but you have others in your life more than willing and able."

I had her say "My dad is a jerk" five times, and with each repeat, she sounded more and more centered.

I then told her to wait for her husband to come home and tell him that he is enough to fill her up, and that she didn't need her dad to morph into father of the year in order to feel good about life.

The next day I got this email from her: "When my husband got home, I spoke with him, and he said, 'Did you call Dr. Laura?' We laughed, of course. A huge weight has been lifted off of my shoulders after I talked to you. My dad is a hard worker and I respect some aspects of him, but in most cases, he is a jerk and I have come to terms with that now. Thank you."

DR. LAURA SAYS:

Accepting reality opens your heart and mind to peace and joy.

Divorce Rarely Has a Fairy Tale Ending

Children's fairy tales—take *Cinderella*, for example—are riddled with stories of the evil stepmother. In reality, evil stepmothers are probably the exception.

Nonetheless, second marriages with children have a divorce rate of more than 70 percent.

What are the problems? For beginners, the children don't pick their parent's new spouse. They usually don't have a say. While it may be the agenda of the adults to have everyone love each other, that doesn't necessarily happen.

Things can be fine when daddy has a new "friend." But when the marriage deal is sealed, all hell breaks loose. That's when the "friend" becomes an omnipresent interloper with power.

Stepmothers who are wonderfully loving might actually have a harder time making the new family arrangement work. Why?

Because all that warmth often causes strong inner emotional conflict in the stepchildren. On one hand they enjoy feeling loved. But at the same time they have a sense of loyalty to their biological mother—who at times does not give them the green light to get along with daddy's new wife.

Rivalry behaviors between ex-wife and stepmother can be ferocious and relentless. The stepmother feels the ex-wife is treading on her new turf when in reality the stepmother is the invader in a preexisting family. Mr. Wonderful is in the middle, wanting to make his new marriage work while trying to keep the mother of his children happy so that she will interfere less with his relationship with the children. This is often a lose-lose situation.

When mothers call me about divorcing, I always warn them that if they divorce, their ex-husband will have visitation and the ability to bring new women into their children's lives.

I ask them to think strongly about whether their desire for divorce is ultimately worth the cost. I frankly say the same to men, warning that they will in effect become "uncle," while some other man is with the children full-time. This realization often helps people think about repairing the marriage instead of ending it.

In Barbara Dafoe Whitehead's classic book, *The Divorce Culture*, she points out that all these factors and more make second marriages difficult and contribute to their high divorce rate. That means that kids from already-broken homes go through it again.

I recommend that people neither date nor marry someone who has minor children. The stress and difficulties are supremely difficult to overcome.

Does it sometimes work out? Yes, of course, but that's the exception.

DR. LAURA SAYS:

If you had a 70 percent chance of dying in a fiery plane crash, would you choose to get on that plane?! I have never heard anyone answer yes. So don't put children in that situation, either.

Divorce Can Be Selfish

In my research, on my radio show, and in my personal appearances, many people share the challenges of marriage and family. One typical concern comes up time and time again: the problem of taking care of children at home by a parent when there's been a divorce, which generally results in day care and a working custodial parent—usually the mother.

There are two concepts I believe are "truths": (1) that the quality of love and attention of a parent is superior to that of hired help (nanny, day-care worker, babysitter), and (2) that children have the best opportunity to grow up healthy, happy, and functional with a married mommy and daddy. That some people can't or won't provide those things doesn't change their importance to a child.

I remember when my husband and I decided to become parents. I specifically asked: "Is there any reason you can see after all the years we've known each other that you might decide to divorce me? Because if there is even an ounce of ambivalence in either of us to this marital commitment, we shouldn't have a child and risk the quality of their lives."

Sadly, too many folks don't consider these issues out loud before they marry and before they have children. When the stresses of life pile up, their individual or mutual ability to live by their vows evaporates.

Of course, the bond may be broken irrevocably when violence, addictions, and/or infidelities occur.

However, most marital breakups seem to stem more from people having long-term individual problems with being able to love, show compassion, share, and be understanding and giving, while acting instead as though they were "sleeping with the enemy."

I deal every day on my radio program with just such seemingly insurmountable barriers to a happy marriage—only to help people better understand the inner fears and egos that are getting in the way of their happiness.

I am convinced that the vast majority of divorces don't need to happen and that most people do not find a pot of happy gold at the end of their marital dissolution. That's because their original problems haven't been solved.

It is, for example, typical of people to live their adult lives in the context of their childhoods instead of the here and now. I recently discerned one caller's problem as her fear that, if she were all open and loving with her husband, it would mean that she no longer could protect herself from him. The "him" is her dad, who was brutal to her mom, and not her husband, who she admitted is a very wonderful man.

Without an intervention, like our conversation, her "coldness" might have driven her husband to leave her. The other threat was that her coldness would lead him to start behaving unkindly, to which she would say to herself, "See?! I was right not to trust!"

Staying together out of respect for the needs of a child to have the bonds to both parents and a role model for the potential blessings of his or her future is a perfect broth in which to create a family soup. Joint motivation in the best interest of something outside yourselves is a great starting point.

The next step is introspection, combined with treating the other person "as if" things were the way we've only dreamed of. That means a kind word, a touch of a hand, a kiss on the cheek, a favor done without asking, a small blanket on his or her feet, a suggestion that your spouse relax in the tub while you get some household task done, or any act of generosity. You will feel the better for doing it. These acts are worth more than a million "discussions." The response you get will motivate you to be and feel happier about being there.

Staying together is not enough, but it is the blessed opportunity to bring more joy and peace to your own life, your spouse, the children, and your family as a whole. Your extended family's support is always a blessing, so saying nice things about your spouse to both sides of the family generates even more positive feelings all around.

While you are "staying together," your children benefit from both mom and dad; don't have to compete with your new "love interests" and other children you inherit or create; don't have to live two lives; don't have to exist in the middle of perpetual rancor; and don't have to resort to drugs, alcohol, sex, and other misbehaviors to get attention or get back at you.

All of the preceding won't make your divorced life much of a pleasure, if you think about it.

DR. LAURA SAYS:

Yes, short of dangerous or destructive conditions, I vote for staying together for the sake of the children because everybody wins IF you do it right.

REFLECTIONS

When people call me about their marriage, it is generally to complain about their spouses! I have to work very hard to help them see their contribution to the mess. What makes that so important is the following: If YOU contributed to the problem, then YOU actually DO HAVE POWER to help turn things around . . . if it isn't too late.

Part Two

PARENTING

Don't hide from questions. Don't lie for the sake
of a false sense of security. Children need
to know—age appropriately—the realities of life.

Morals, principles, and values are not annoying blocks to a happy life. Quite the opposite. These age-old concepts actually protected the vulnerable—women and children—from situations that cause pain and suffering.

Back in the day, a man without a job or enough in the bank to support a wife and kids could not get through the front door of a girl's house to see her because her father would be at the door telling him to come back when he was solvent and responsible. These days, parents act like they are confused and impotent. This does nothing to help inexperienced young people learn to navigate through life. Future generations are surely getting the message: Shack up in a relationship where anything goes, postpone marriage, and hope for the best. Today's parents must lead by example. Does it have to be said?

CHAPTER FIVE

Reality Check for Parents

Parenting is an experience that forces you to think about something outside yourself! Unfortunately, parenting over the last decade or two has collapsed into inundating children with electronic equipment and outside activities to the loss of not only family time, but the opportunity to actually parent children. Instead of teaching morals, values, principles, and ethics, guilty parents (divorced/remarried/new kids/two-career parents, etc.) superindulge their children and give up being parents— becoming friends or barely custodians.

Older parents crying about their adult kids not having much to do with them other than getting money or other perks will frequently admit that they spoiled their kids and made them brats who don't respect them. When I ask why they did this, it turns out to be total selfishness and laziness.

Parents have a moral obligation to sacrifice for the well-being of their children and not the reverse. A famous and former female anchor for the *Today Show* interviewed me and extolled the virtues of her incredibly busy schedule as good role modeling for her children, who are very proud of her. I shot back with, "Well, we aren't supposed to have kids so we have a cheering section."

Ooooohh.

What Children Need

Based on my experiences as a psychotherapist and radio talk show host dealing with people's pain for many years, I think I have a handle on what children need from their parents. To me, an optimal childhood would look something like this:

1. A mother and a father. The growing trend of single people thinking it is their right to have a child regardless of the immutable needs of children is despicable. To intentionally rob a child of a father or a mother for selfish purposes is to treat a child like a possession rather than a complex being. It is sad enough when a parent is lost by death, but by divorce or "none at all" is a painful insult felt in a personal way by the child who forever experiences a significant loss.

2. A mother and a father who are not addicted to drugs or alcohol.

3. A mother and a father who are committed to the marriage and who do not give in to inappropriate fantasies (Internet porn or illicit relationships) or behaviors (flirtations or adultery) or selfish whims (spending an excessive amount of time on hobbies or with buddies).

4. A mother and a father who sacrifice personal concerns and opportunities for the welfare of the family; who do not use or abuse the commitment of the other for personal gain.

5. A mother and a father who work out childcare so that children are raised by a loving, involved parent instead of hired help or in institutionalized day care.

6. A mother and a father who take responsibility for their own emotional and psychological issues (childhood abuse, an over-enmeshed original family, etc.), and do not permit these internal aches and pains to damage their ability to properly function in the context of spouse and parent.

7. A mother and a father who do not compete with each other for power, perks, or popularity—but who see themselves "as one" and hold the well-being of the other spouse before their own.

8. A mother and a father who, if divorced, do not start new families with new children so that their original children are only visitors in their new lives.

9. A mother and a father who take the time to teach their children moral and ethical values and admirable practical life strategies, not only by their words, but by their role modeling.

10. A mother and a father who teach their children responsibility through consequences—who do not simply protect and rescue their children or take their position against what is right and just.

DR. LAURA SAYS:

Take pride in raising your own kids: Purpose and meaning are the reward.

Caring for Our Kids—My Five Challenges to Parents

I have been licensed as a marriage and family therapist in California for over two decades (although no longer in private practice) after extensive training at USC's Human Relations Center. I have taught Therapy Techniques and Abnormal Psychology in the Graduate Psychology Program of Pepperdine University.

Between the hundreds of calls, letters, emails, and faxes that I handle on a weekly basis, I would say that I have a pretty good finger on the pulse of our society.

I'm scared. More and more, folks seem to have a difficult time discerning wrong, bad, or evil, and an even more difficult time being willing to face, challenge, or obliterate it.

How and why has this happened? Media have the biggest responsibility. With the proliferation of media outlets and the mainstreaming of ever-relaxing moral standards, children and young adults feel free from the "constraining oppression" of religious and parental authority and good sense.

In popular culture, in movies, and in the vast amount of programs available 24/7, the message is clear: Sex anywhere, anytime, with anyone is okay. Or sex anywhere, anytime, but with a spouse is not okay. Follow up with kids out of wedlock being okay, but staying home with kids to love and nurture them while the other spouse is at work is not okay.

This confuses people, and confused people who don't have the strong support of an intact family and religious foundation tend to push the limits and hurt themselves and others.

The women's movement continues to be quite destructive to the core instinct of mothers by extolling the virtues of independent, powerful, accomplished, working mothers even when there are babies and minor children to consider. It is with respect to the welfare of children that I see the biggest decline in concern, much less responsibility. In one day I read news stories telling me:

- Yet another infant suffocated in the heat of a locked car because the parent was too distracted by work and parking issues to remember that a child was in the back seat. How can you forget your own flesh and blood?
- Webcams allow a mother to check on her baby. "You wouldn't believe how much stress this takes off (the mother)," said an "infant instructor." Can the webcam love, caress, feed, hold, play, and bond with the baby?

- A nursing journal extols the virtue of giving antidepressants to children, complete with a joyous post-medicine/therapy photo of a 10-year-old girl who looks delighted—despite her parents' divorce. How about we drug the parents into treating each other well enough to avoid her emotional collapse?

Every day I receive calls from people who "don't see it" or "don't really care" about the impact that their life's choices have on their children. And what really gets me is how matter-of-fact they are in presenting themselves.

An example: women callers who feel perfectly justified moving their children away from a good father after a divorce to "find themselves," be near their parents, have a new environment, be with a new boyfriend, shack up, or get remarried.

As I've said before, one of the most egregious behaviors of divorced parents is remarrying and raising someone else's children—or producing new children—while their own children are relegated to "visitation."

This amounts to one of the most alarming trends of any culture: the diminished regard and commitment to its weakest, most dependent members—children.

The degree of self-centeredness, the unwillingness to label wrong as being wrong, the impulsive desire to "feel" momentary pleasure to the exclusion of responsibilities and obligations—all these spell disaster for any civilization.

Here is my five-point challenge to you:

1. Get a notebook out, and while you watch your shows (comedy or drama), jot down what the underlying or overt messages are—intended or not. Analyze the plots and dialogues for "teachings" and then note which of those teachings you believe are good/bad for you, your children, society at large.

2. Be willing to get into a debate (or even argument) with anyone over the issue of right and wrong being "in the eye of the beholder." Be willing to stand up, for example, and say that a baby shower for an unwed mother is not an appropriate celebration; planning to fill in for the missing father is the concern.

3. Start posting comments on local and national platforms, standing up for the innocent and the dependent, risking, of course, being called mean for saying, "Nanny cams in homes don't hug and love a child—they only alert a parent to potential violence toward their child."

4. Get a stack of books like *Living a Rich Life as a Stay-at-Home Mom: How to Build a Secure Financial Foundation for You and Your Children.*

5. Attend church/synagogue regularly to reinforce eternal and universal values and to get involved in community projects to go do the right thing.

DR. LAURA SAYS:

Jeff, a listener, wrote: "When my wife was on maternity leave after having our first son, we started putting more thought into our priorities. It was clear our son was worthy of any sacrifice." Nice.

Uncaring Parent, Uncaring Kids

Over the years, I have noticed many societal trends—mostly bad. These include the growing prevalence of hooking up, shacking up, having babies out of wedlock, using abortions as birth control, and lacking commitment.

Lately, more and more parents are calling me complaining that their adult children never call, never visit, never convene on holidays, and don't remember birthdays.

When I ask the obvious first question—"What do you believe is the cause of this disregard?—I always get back, "I don't know."

Well, I do know. If your adult children don't feel bonded or give a whit about you, it is probably your own fault.

I am amazed at how parents deny that their behavior and decisions impacted their children in ways that made those children disconnect emotionally. Folks have children, and instead of raising them, turn them over to day-care facilities, nannies, and babysitters. Then they divorce, expecting their children to go away, along with the furniture. Children end up going back and forth between warring parents and never put down roots.

Additionally, we have become a culture of victims. This trend has to do with mental illness diagnoses that clearly take the focus away from children. Everyone is bipolar or has PTSD or ADHD. All these diagnoses—which have ballooned in numbers over the past two or so decades—disrupt families and take attention and caretaking away from children.

Of course, there are those who do really suffer from these mental illnesses, and that is truly heartbreaking. However, I believe there have been trendy diagnoses that have more to do with self-centered parents, pharmaceutical company profits, and income for therapists than with reality.

When parents have not made their children's needs a priority, why do they expect their children to do anything other than return that lack of favor?

So many older mothers who call complaining that their adult children make no effort to see them just won't accept that they earned it.

Some adult children are so ambivalent about their parents that they don't even want to attend their mother's or father's funeral. I have had to support many adult children in their decision to "stay away" from a bad parent.

I do remind them, however, that even though their parent was not motivated by obligation and responsibility, that unless that parent was dangerous or destructive, they should make sure the parent's basic needs for food, housing, and medications are met, even if they pay someone else to do it.

DR. LAURA SAYS:

Do not let the fact that you had a bad parent impact the quality of your own character. Appropriately administered compassion is the decent thing to do.

Love Being a Parent

I frankly love those "priceless" credit card commercials, where they point out the price of a few things, and then zero in on something like a parent and child having quality time together, the sentiment being "some things are priceless—for everything else, there's Mastercard." That commercial is easy to love because it differentiates between commodities and love, familial intimacy, emotional fulfillment, and the beauty of family.

I recently read a news blog that stated, "Stay-at-Home Moms Deserve High Pay, Analysis Shows." It suggests that the average housewife-mom's work should bring $131,471 annually (40 hours per week plus 60 hours "overtime"), with a job description that ranges from chef to van driver, cook to teacher, and so forth. They're right! If you were to farm out each and every daily task of a housewife-mom to a "professional," it surely would mount up to at least $100,000.

I then started to think of the breadwinner-husband-dad. He gets a salary from an employer, which is typically all brought home for the family. He doesn't, however, get paid for the time he spends in traffic commuting, doing the lawn, fixing the cars, painting the house, handling the plumbing issues, taking out the garbage, dealing with discipline issues, tutoring mathematics and computers, coaching little league and/or soccer, hanging with the kids while mom has "girl time," figuring out budgets and taxes, and dealing with his in-laws.

Happily, the news piece ended with a quote from a stay-home mom with a two-year-old daughter and four-month-old son: "I'm giving 150 percent of myself to them many hours a day. You cannot attach a dollar value to the time that you spent nurturing you children . . ."

A "Proud Mom in California" wrote to me recently about how ashamed she is of herself. Her eight-year-old daughter had a field trip. The day before the trip, the mom had started to complain to her husband about going: the bouncy bus, noisy kids, and the grueling, long, boring, trapped day ahead of her. The morning of the trip, she looked at her husband with an "attitude" and said, "You owe me one!"

"The trip down," she wrote:

> . . . was actually not so bad. My daughter and I played tic tac toe, hang man, and did a little finger knitting as kids from the other seats watched and seemed interested in our activities. The nature hike gave her a blister on her foot, for which I quickly whipped out a Band-Aid . . . and then another for the thorn she got in her finger.

On the way home, my daughter cuddled up to me and rested on my arm. We finally got home and my strong, independent little eight-year-old said, "Mom, I liked you being there." Later that night I turned to my husband and said, 'Thanks for making me go . . . I owe you one!'"

Many do farm out all those parenting responsibilities and joys to day-care workers, nannies, and babysitters, having "hired help" do everything from birthday parties, to potty training, to teaching kids how to ride a bike at $60/hour. Many parents are grateful not to have to hassle with the exasperating confrontations that are a normal part of raising children. The natural consequence, however, is no loving bond between parent and child—which is a terrible loss for both.

Too much of our culture is wrapped up in becoming an idol or a millionaire; certain things *are simply priceless*. Here are 10 priceless reasons to be a parent:

MOMS get to:

1. Be involved with all the children's activities, and their nutrition, safety, and experiences.
2. Build emotional and psychological bonds of love that will last a lifetime.
3. Determine a child's educational experience and development of morals and values.
4. Create an environment of warmth, sustenance, and peace for the whole family.
5. Experience pride in being the focal point of the whole family.

DADS get to:

1. Feel pride in purposeful work, beyond gratification, because they are working FOR *their wives and children.*
2. Feel connected to their wives through joint focus on their children.
3. Enjoy passing down knowledge and skills to their children.
4. Benefit from the contentment and harmony that having a home and family generally brings.
5. Benefit from living for their families, because men generally strive more and are more successful, happy, and healthy when they have families.

DR. LAURA SAYS:

Parenting is priceless.

REFLECTIONS

Interesting question: Should you let your children win at competitions against you (board games, sports) so that they build self-esteem? The answer is no. Self-esteem does not come from winning. Self-esteem comes from being proud of yourself: your courage, compassion, and tenacity. And you should be proud when you adhere to values, overcome obstacles, and face challenges. Did I mention winning? No, I didn't. As a matter of fact, children build greater self-esteem when they learn to lose with grace than when they win. Here's what parents have to tell their children: "Sometimes you win, and sometimes someone else wins. You have to be gracious to your competitors whether you win or lose. You have to be kind, supportive, and complimentary to your teammates even while losing." When you play with your kids, play to win; but handicap yourself in some way to make things fair. When my son was younger I taught him the tricks of playing Scrabble. I would help him with spelling and how to get the most points. I helped less and less as he got better and better. I never let him win. Now he has become the only human being on the planet to ever beat me at Scrabble. And I don't believe that would have happened had he not been forced to work at it (with me mentoring him). The first time he beat me, he knew that he really won and that he earned it himself. If your child yells, screams, pouts, says bad things, and generally acts like a poor sport, explain what behavior you expect—and clarify that when you don't see the behavior your expect, win or lose, you will be disappointed and there will be consequences.

CHAPTER SIX

For Women Only

Although no longer practicing, my family and I converted years ago to Orthodox Judaism. People unfamiliar with religious practices would comment that the religion was very sexist by not permitting women to participate in much of the serious religious activities such as going up to the Torah during services. I came to understand early on that the mentality is that women are already more sublimely associated with God and the men had to be elevated from their baser instincts with the rituals and rules. If you look at the history of the world, that makes total sense!

However, with feminism, women have been denied the beauty of being on a pedestal and their sublime roles as mother and wife and garnering the respect due a LADY. I have joked on the air that I, a black belt in martial arts, could knock down many doors, but I will stand forever to have a gentleman simply open one. He feels special doing it—especially if you are gracious about it—and you feel special having it done for you.

That's why I always joke (?) that I am waiting for Rhett Butler to call on me.

Wife, Mother—VIP

"I am not important."

That was the astounding cry of a caller to my radio show. She is a woman who put her career aside after she married so that she could make her house a home, raise her children, and be a good wife to her lucky husband.

It was distressing to hear a woman say that her life has no value because she is not "famous or successful." I explained that her children will always cherish her love, devotion, kindness, commitment, sweetness, fun, and sensitivity. Then I related a story to her of one person in my life who is centrally important to the building of my character. It is a person I never met, my maternal aunt, Lucia.

During World War II, Lucia and my mother were sisters in the small town of Gorizia on the border of what was Yugoslavia and Italy. Their parents ran a restaurant, visited each evening by members of the German High Command. Lucia would sometimes overhear the Nazis discussing their plans, and she would convey this information to the Italian underground.

At some point my aunt decided to actually join the underground group to fight fascist and Nazi evils. She was 20 at the time. She never became 21.

The day after she joined, the group was rounded up. She was lined up against a wall with the other heroes and shot.

I don't even know what my Aunt Lucia looked like, but she has always been the most important influence in my life. She was not famous, nor was she considered successful during her lifetime.

But the central point here is that importance can be defined in many ways. Influencing others is an important role even if it is not a famous one.

Every step in your life, you touch other people for good or for not. Each contact makes an impact on that other person, who then impacts others. It is a chain reaction. There is almost no way to be unimportant as long as you consider the well-being of others important. Whenever you touch another's life with benevolence, you become important to the world.

Consider yourself a stone thrown across the water of a pond. Watch the infinite ripples caused by one, single, seemingly unimportant, small pebble.

DR. LAURA SAYS:

Contributing to the healthy growth, development, and functioning of other human beings is of supreme importance—and the greatest thing to which we can aspire.

Best Moms Put Kids Above All Else

I live near the ocean in California, which means I can view huge pods of dolphins and small groups of whales as they migrate or search for food.

Once, a killer whale flew out of the water and landed full force on a 20-foot fishing boat. The fishermen had gotten between a calf and her mother. I actually had the opportunity to see the boat and was amazed at what the force of a falling orca means to the average fishing boat. One of the fishermen ended up in the hospital.

I remember being so incredibly impressed with the passion and courage of the mother and the fact she was willing to give her life to protect her offspring.

Let me jump directly from that scenario to a caller on my program. This woman told me her parents had been divorced for quite a while and her dad has always had rage behavior. Not only would he yell and scream and carry on, but he would get physically violent with his family. She is now married and has two small children.

She told him that she didn't want to see him because his violence was unpredictable and out of control. "But," she went on, "I feel bad about him not seeing my kids. After all, he is my father."

I just about flew out of my skin. I told her in no uncertain terms that this was not the behavior of a good mother, but of a little girl who is willing to sacrifice the safety and well-being of her children to stay connected to her dangerous father on the off chance that he will someday change and love her.

A mother is there to protect and nurture and not to make decisions for her children based on her own emotional needs. With respect to offspring, I vote for instinctive behavior and not decisions made of selfishness or weakness.

These considerations are far-ranging. I've spoken to way too many mothers who married or shacked up with some guy knowing full well that her children didn't like him or his children. And there are mothers who marry again and make new babies while their children go back and forth from dad's home, experiencing the pain of visiting mom raising some other children. Others work full-time and neglect their kids because they love their career. It goes on.

Sometimes we have to make hard decisions. But a good mother always does what is best for her children. It is especially sad when a family breaks up, but less so when it is in the best interest of the children to do so.

> ## DR. LAURA SAYS:
> The best mothers protect their children above personal needs and fears.

Why Is Everyone So Afraid to Say, "This Is Wrong!"?

Two days before Christmas a few years ago, while I was busy delivering Christmas goodies around my small town, a woman came up to me, ostensibly for a greeting. She immediately began to attack me: "I actually listened to you say that women who give birth to out-of-wedlock children are sluts. I am one of those women, and I am not a slut. You have brought shame into what should have been a lovely experience. I didn't abort!"

Stupidly, I tried to correct her, letting her know that I have not called such women sluts. I also tried to congratulate her for not aborting, while reminding her that adoption to a mom and dad in a convenant marriage was also an option—but I couldn't get a word in edgewise. She just kept yelling while I was trying to establish a dialogue. I finally lost it (yes, I can get as frustrated as the next person!) and said, "Okay, you are a slut—for robbing a child of a father!" Actually, she did take a breath on that one, but she started ranting all over again, finishing with, "I'm writing a book, and you are in it."

As I walked away I remembered a television experience I had while promoting one of my books in Oregon. There was a live studio audience, and during the Q&A period one young lady stood up and said that I should not "put down" unwed mothers because her mother was one, and she turned out fine. I immediately asked her if she planned to make sure that her children would not grow up in an intact home with a married mother and father. She sputtered a moment, said "No," then realizing what she'd said, started rambling on again about how wonderful her mother is and how there was no loss to her. I queried again: "If there was no loss for you, why don't you want to plan to have out-of-wedlock children and give them the same wonderful experience you had?"

I am very impressed with women who, when caught by biology because of irresponsible behavior, do not have an abortion in order to solve the inconvenient or embarrassing problem. These women are heroes. I do believe that the best option, however, for these children is adoption to a stable, loving, two-parent, married, mom-and-dad family. Without that, they suffer from no father; a string of mother's boyfriends/shack-ups; the risk of being a third wheel with their father's other family attachments and commitments; and ultimately, instability, which leads to insecurities.

Women are becoming less and less competent in relationships, thanks to the anti-male emphasis of the influential feminist mentality in our society. Some are "choosing" (and that's become a sacred word that eliminates judgment) to become mothers without a father on purpose. These women, in my opinion, are so self-centered, thoughtless, insensitive, and uncaring about the well-being of their child (in the face of voluminous information about the price such children pay) that they can be considered as doing evil.

One such woman in my town became a celebrity for intentionally having four children with implanted embryos. The town went gaga over helping her with money and baby things. I went on the radio and condemned her actions, as well as the thoughtless, nonjudgmental townsfolk. I never mentioned her name (respecting privacy and not wanting to hurt the children)—but the story ended up on Oprah and Bill O'Reilly's TV show.

Oprah became her advocate, which disgusted me. It became all about the woman's desires, her rights, her choice, her freedoms and—except for my show—never about the well-being of the children. A year later, the local newspaper told the story of her meeting some guy through Oprah's show and shacking up with him for a year on his ranch. She was quoted as saying this was only temporary because she had other plans.

So here you have it. She never accepted any responsibility for the feelings and needs of her kids. They would bond with this man and then lose him. They don't even live in one place. Why is everyone so afraid to say, "This is wrong!"?

DR. LAURA SAYS:

Well, I'm not afraid. This is wrong! And if it takes women being called "sluts" again to stop this wholesale emotional and psychological abuse of children, I'll start saying that and splatter "shame" everywhere I can.

Grandmothers Offer Grand Support

One recurrent topic on my daily radio program has to do with the grandmother "issue." Here's the typical scenario: The matriarch has two children, one female and one male. In their respective marriages, they each have children. The wife of the male child is quite disconcerted that grandma seems to favor the children of her daughter over those of her son.

At first, I always ask, "Can you think of any reason that your mother-in-law might be more comfortable at the other home?" The daughter-in-law caller will frequently say no at first, and then mention moments of tension as they might disagree about style of parenting and there may exist tensions in the relationship between mother and daughter-in-law.

Bingo.

When a mother has a married daughter, they have been in a relationship for decades. There may be some typical ups and downs, but they simply feel very connected. They are also pretty much in agreement with the concepts of child-rearing, styles of family relating, mutual expectations, and problem resolution. They also have worked out how to relate personally.

The daughter-in-law is the woman who takes over her mother-in-law's position as the important woman in the man's life. They have not known each other for decades, and they differ in backgrounds, life experiences, and expectations. A healthy, reasonable grandmother understands this intellectually, but feels the "shove" anyway. She generally feels she has to walk on eggshells with her daughter-in-law lest she say or do something that triggers any sense of offense or challenge . . . and then the husband is placed squarely in the middle.

I have been somewhat amused by how many daughters-in-law complain about how grandma takes care of the kids, because she married the man that grandma raised. It is curious that a woman can love the man, but not the woman who had a lot to do in making him the man she loves.

Misunderstandings and hurt feelings between women in general happen so easily—especially when husband/son/grandchildren are in the mix. I tell the grandmother to smile a lot and agree so that her son is not torn apart by the two important women in his life—and so that grandma has access to the grandchildren.

I remind people that love may or may not develop, but respect and kindness should go both ways for everyone's sake. For goodness sakes, just be polite!

Communication is so important. Don't be negative. Grandma should never say, "You never let me do anything." Instead, she should try, "I understand you might not feel comfortable with me taking them for the day. How can I make this feel good to you?"

Never think you are going to win points by using criticism, threats, or general negativity. Grandmas are very important to the health of the marriage and the well-being of the children. We just can't have enough support to get through the trials and tribulations and surprises life throws us.

DR. LAURA SAYS:

Both sides have issues. Simply being kind, thoughtful, and polite goes a long way to making life easier for everyone.

I Take This Mother Thing Personally

I was a victim of the '60s feminista mentality of "power to the estrogen!" So I spent most of my early adult years trying very hard to be successful at all costs, not have any man treat me like a "babe," and also seeing wife and mother as a great cop-out to the cause of feminine enlightenment.

Now I measure success by having a purpose to my work that benefits others. Now a day without being called a "babe" is a day without sunshine. And being a wife and mother has taught me the blessings of living outside myself—a cure for basic, adolescent self-centeredness.

Every day, I open my radio program by saying, "I am my kid's mom," because I feel it is the most important thing I've ever done: bring new life into the world and try my best to love and direct that life to be a functioning, contributing, decent, happy human being. I don't know what to say about those difficult teenage years. Fortunately, they are now a blur.

Even though my son is grown and is in the military, I still begin each hour with the reference to motherhood as a reminder to all mothers that this part of their lives is not the drudgery or feminist cop-out side of them—but the side that defines the uniqueness of our gender. Moms are the spiritual and emotional center of the family.

But here's the sticky part, as measured by the anger demonstrated toward women who choose to actually raise their own children as stay-at-home moms. Unless a woman is mentally ill or addled by drug abuse, it's hard to imagine that her loving arms and tender words could be replaced with hired help: nannies, day-care workers, or babysitters. In fact, I doubt any of you reading this would choose a nanny, day-care center, or babysitter for yourself instead of a warm mommy, would you?

Now for those mothers who can't or won't raise their own children, I am sad for what both child and mother miss: all the firsts, the sillies, the trials and tribulations, the explanations of life and bugs, the comfort and safety, the adventures, the challenges, and the stories both will remember for the rest of their lives.

I have no desire to get into the mommy wars about whether hired help is sufficient intellectually and emotionally. I think that's kind of silly. I've never really understood why any mother would want to believe that she is replaceable: that her voice, her hands, her smile, her attention, and her love could be matched by someone who may have taken a child development class.

My book *In Praise of Stay-at-Home Moms* is not an argument—it is a testimonial to those women who sacrifice careers and free time to raise their children. The book deals with the difficult transition from work to home, the insults and arguments from those who tell them they're wasting their time and education, and the challenges of combining mothering with the myriad responsibilities of running a household.

The book is filled with inspirational and unbelievably touching letters from women who have made the transition from a life of "me" to a life of "we."

Here's one meaningful example:

Tonight, as I lay next to my four-year-old daughter, rubbing her back, singing a song, helping her fall asleep, she looked at me with tears in her eyes, grabbed my face with both hands, and said with such love and conviction, 'You are my lullaby, mommy!' I cried then and there, and the tears continued to flow as she slept in my arms. No, I don't get to have a latte at 10, go to lunch with co-workers, and out for drinks after work. I am not being overseen by someone who gives me performance-based raises and praise. Instead, I am in the most beautiful and profound position I could every hold: I am my daughter's lullaby.

DR. LAURA SAYS:

Until my son hit 18, I always introduced myself on my radio program by saying, "I am my kid's mom." At a book signing I once had a college girl ask me why, with all my degrees and awards, I introduced myself that way. She was to report back to her women's studies class. I laughed and said, "Because it is the most important and wonderful thing I have ever done." She looked confused. Wish I could have been a fly on the wall in her class to hear the discussion when she reported back!

Voices in the Darkness

I receive emails like this one every week:

> Dear Dr. Laura,
>
> My husband and I are expecting our 3rd child next sum-
> mer. I joined a birth club group on a popular pregnancy
> website to hear of others' experiences. On Christmas Eve
> I stumbled on a post from a woman complaining of her
> family's reaction to her decision to purposely get pregnant
> by a man she was not intending to marry or even date.
> She believed at 24 she was financially and emotionally sta-
> ble enough to provide for a baby. A father wasn't needed.
> However, her family is not supportive and she is appalled
> by their judgment.
>
> Obviously, she's now looking for sympathy online.
> The feminist movement has unfortunately taught young
> women like her that men are not needed and that farm-
> ing your child out to hired help is OK. I responded rather
> harshly, but a point needed to be made. I said: "You've
> made an extremely selfish decision to have a baby without
> a dad. I feel bad for your child."
>
> Keep up the hard work, Dr. Laura.
>
> Sincerely, Natasha

The core of human existence is the family. The feminist anti-
wife/anti-mother mentality has done more to destroy the family
than any other influence. Feminism has supported women having
meaningless sex, ripping babies from their body to die, and ignor-
ing the significance of fathers in the lives, minds, and hearts of
children. It eschews marriage as slavery and hates everything that
is truly feminine.

I am stunned by the growing number of calls from young women to my radio program who seem clueless about why they are so desperately unhappy after having multiple children with multiple men after shack-ups and failed "relationships."

When I suggest that these bad decisions have led to their misery, many of them actually seem surprised.

Why? Because today's social norms support chaos, impulsiveness, and immediate gratification. Those same social norms largely disrespect religion, moral obligations, responsibilities, sacrifice, and selflessness.

It's all very depressing, but wives and mothers like Natasha provide hope for us all, showing that at least some people get it.

DR. LAURA SAYS:

When Natasha tells me to "keep up the hard work," it is humbling to say the least. She reminds me that enough of our positive, albeit rogue, notes brought together may someday make a symphony.

Never Underestimate the Value of Being a Stay-at-Home Mom

Here's a story from one of my listeners who spoke up in her karate class to a single 20-year-old woman who got pregnant by the instructor.

The couple married, and the young mother is now going to school and putting the infant in day care. Watching the girl with her child, my listener, a parent herself, picked up on how disinterested the mother seemed to be.

My listener told her that she is "hurting her precious baby by putting her in babysitting while she goes to school, and that she is the best mom for her baby girl."

You'd think that compliment—being told you're the best for your child—would be met with happy tears. Nope. The girl went ballistic on her. My listener is not sorry she tried to refocus the young woman toward mothering instead of just getting on with her life in spite of having a child.

After reading the email on my radio program, I asked people to send me their perspective on whether the listener was right in giving her unsolicited opinion when it was sincerely intended to benefit a child.

The responses ranged from "She should have kept her mouth closed" to "I wish someone would have told me sooner that it was the right thing to do (become a full-time, stay-at-home mommy)."

One writer bemoaned not having the "courage to say what needs to be said" with a similar situation in her own family.

The most compelling argument I received about standing up for motherhood was this: "I absolutely do not think she needs to apologize to anyone. How frequently we are bombarded by friends, even family and the media, that being a career woman is much preferable to being a stay-at-home mom. Do they ever consider how this tramples the feelings of children of at-home mothers? Has anyone ever apologized for that?" That is so right.

When you are trying to say something that people don't want to hear, tone and technique are important. Telling them "you are hurting your child" won't win you any friends. It works better to say something like: "It's great that you're continuing with school, but every moment your child spends with you impacts your child's sense of safety and love, and you may be underestimating that. Being a mom myself, I know it is exhausting and frustrating—and the best thing I've ever done. If you'd like me to help you figure this out so you can be with your child more ..."

Hopefully, your words will make people ponder.

DR. LAURA SAYS:

Every human being would rather be raised by a loving mother than a nanny, babysitter, or day-care workers. Look in the mirror—tell me that isn't so for you.

REFLECTIONS

I want to end this section with a letter from Lee, a listener:

> I wanted to let you know of a proud moment that happened recently. I was at a baby shower with my grandma who will be 90 in a few months. We were talking about being a stay-at-home mom and she told me that staying home is something that I will never regret.
>
> My cousin, who works full time and rarely sees her kids except on the weekend, jumped in and said to me, "I don't know how you do it. I was getting ready this morning and my two kids were all over me and wouldn't leave me alone." To which my grandma said, "That's because you are never there. All they want is your attention and love. You should be ashamed for complaining that the children you birthed want and need your attention. They only have one Mom. Remember that!"

She probably didn't wish to remember that. Very sad. That woman will probably call me one day when she is old and alone and complain that her kids don't talk to her and never seem to have time to visit. Sad.

CHAPTER SEVEN

Discipline

Whoever has the responsibility has the power—parents need to understand this and take it seriously and convey the same to their children. Without learning this concept, children will never become responsible adults.

Five Ways to Teach Your Kids Responsibility

A five-year-old boy called my radio program to ask me how he can stop fighting with his parents. He said, "When I want to do things and my mom won't let me, I want to do it anyway, and I get frustrated, so I fight with her about it."

Julian, remember, is only five years old, and that's a good excuse for not yet understanding the concepts of responsibility and power. I then carefully explained to him about how one attains the power to do what one wishes:

Your parents have to completely take care of you. There are rewards that come along with all that responsibility. One is that you get respect, Julian, and you must show your parents respect for all they do for you by not fighting and arguing with them.

Another reward is that you, through taking on responsibilities, get to make the rules and the decisions. That means that since they have the responsibility, they get to have the power to make the rules. And, Julian, as you grow up and take on more responsibility, you will get to make certain decisions for yourself. Then, when you are all grown up and on your own in your own home with your own job, you get to make all the decisions for yourself.

Right now, though, you are five years old and your parents are twenty-seven. They have a lot more experience in life and have a lot more responsibility than you do, at five years old. Maybe you could think of learning from them instead of fighting with them? What do you think, Julian?

This little five-year-old boy got it. Although it will continue to be a struggle as he goes through adolescence and teenage years, if his parents continually reaffirm the concept of "responsibility gets you power," he will be okay.

But too few parents teach or reinforce this concept with their children. Hence, we have a generation of young adults who seem to believe that they are entitled to the power . . . and desire their parents to still carry the burden of responsibility for them. Unbelievable but true. I know. I talk to these so-called adults every day. They call me because they are aghast and enraged that they can't live in two worlds simultaneously: one as an independent adult, the other as a dependent child. This does not bode well for America's future.

One young man, 18 years old, told me, "I have a great job since I graduated high school. I make lots of money. I live at home with my parents. They told me that if I want to stay in their home, I have to go to college. I don't want to go to college because then I'd have to give up this great job."

"Well, then, if you want to have the power to make this decision, you'll have to do it from your own apartment," I said.

"I don't make enough money to pay for all those things," he lamented.

"Great job and making lots of money is what you said. Okay. Get two jobs and support yourself; that's how you get to make the decision," I said.

"Do they have the right to tell me what to do?" he asked.

"No, you're an adult male. They don't have the right to tell you what to do. They do have the right to tell you what you can or cannot do from *their home*! You have the right to do what you want from your own home. So, get one," I offered.

"It's not fair," he said.

"Don't you get it?" I asked. "The only reason you have 'a lot of money' is that you don't pay for your own upkeep! You can't even support yourself. Your mommy and daddy take total care of you . . . You can't have it both ways. You have to pick one."

He did not end this conversation satisfied at all. Neither did a young 18-year-old who called because her parents did not like her boyfriend, with whom she lives, and by whom she got pregnant at 17—the pregnancy ending in a miscarriage. She was mad at her parents because they were not going to give her money for living expenses and more schooling.

I said, "Are you kidding? You are with a boy they warned you about, you got pregnant as an unmarried minor—and don't forget that your pregnancy was not just with YOUR CHILD; it was with THEIR FIRST GRANDCHILD—you leave their home to live with this guy, and you expect that they will continue to be financially supporting you as though you were a dependent child?"

These calls are actual and are typical of young people today. What are the causes of this juvenile mentality? Overall, our children from birth have "too much" in spite of "being and doing too little." Guilty parents cave into this because it's just easier than actually raising one's children to become competent adults.

No matter what the age of your children, consider these five points:

1. Teach your children from the earliest age the concept that POWER is a CONSEQUENCE of RESPONSIBIL-ITY—and not a given due simply to desire.
2. Give your child the power to make certain decisions based upon the successful, continuous completion of certain responsibilities—let them see firsthand how they can earn power.
3. Do not indulge your children at any age by rescuing them, bribing them, paying them off for imagined or real guilt of yours (like divorce/remarried guilt), or getting them things to make them "happy."
4. Point out the true value of "things" by how you lead your own life. Talk about the pride you have in earning things . . . the old-fashioned way. Earning, not having, is what makes happiness.
5. Discuss these issues as they come up. Some things may look good, but are they good for you?

DR. LAURA SAYS:

Your job is to turn your children into responsible, independent, functioning adults. Keep that in mind!

Our Kids Need Downtime to Dream Big

I've noticed a disturbing pattern with today's young adults.

It began when a young female caller to my radio show was unable to answer my simple questions: "What is your dream? What is your passion?"

The very next day, another young person had the same issue. At first I said, "I can't believe this. Two folks in two days telling me they don't and never have had a dream!"

Once I heard myself say this out loud, it hit me that it wasn't because they were holding back from expressing themselves. They really didn't have a dream or a passion.

I realized that to have dreams and passions one must have introspective time. Children as well as adults are glued to screens these days: iPads, cell phones, computers, etc. There is no downtime to engage even the most superficial parts of one's awareness, consciousness, intellect, and activity.

A recent study finds that children spend most of their school hours looking at screens—not teachers, not other children, not puzzles, not books, not drawing—just looking at screens.

They say that Sir Isaac Newton was sitting on the grass under a tree when an apple fell and hit him square atop his head. His next thoughts went to the concept of gravity, forever changing the course of science. Right now, the important part of that story is not that he gained an understanding of gravity, but that Newton was doing absolutely nothing when the inspirational thought hit him . . . literally!

Creativity needs "downtime." It needs the brain to be free to wander and make idle associations. The same is true for knowing yourself and your purpose, which ultimately comes from your dreams and passions.

Children used to "dream" of becoming ballerinas, firefighters, physicians, parents, gardeners, chefs, and so on. They would playact their dreams alone and with friends. They would build themselves toward a purpose.

Today children have very little time, space, and direction to have such introspection. Kids are kept busy at all times, in part out of societal pressure, in part for the convenience of their parents, who usually either are overly invested in their careers, or are in the midst of divorces, dating, and remarriage, or are just not highly motivated to spend time with their children.

It is sad that so many children are being groomed to be techno robots who don't know themselves, their dreams, or their passions. I hear them every day: lonely, sad, and lost.

DR. LAURA SAYS:

Children need more time under an apple tree. We all do!

Parents Need to Take Control

I finally figured out the main problem with young people today: parents.

For at least one or two generations, parents have required little of their children while giving them everything.

One family I met with has a mom and dad who are wonderful people. However, the daughter, a preadolescent, had become the tyrant of the family. She was moody and had outbursts of rude, disrespectful, and mean behavior toward her five-year-old brother. As a result, the little boy had become submissive and sullen.

I recommended the following to the mother: At the first sign of her daughter's nasty behavior, eliminate whatever next activity she has scheduled with no warning. Surprise attacks always get everyone's attention. When she yells and tries to bully her way into getting the activity back, warn her that if she continues, the next activity will also be gone.

My conversation with the mother took place one hour before the daughter was to be driven to her basketball game. We stayed in text contact. The first text from mom read: "basketball gone."

She then warned her daughter that any further acting up would be met with the loss of the next activity. Yup, that was lost also. Then, miraculously, the daughter contained herself.

I explained to mom that while it seemed wonderful to make so many activities available for her daughter, the girl took them for granted since she didn't have to earn them in any way. Children today are kept so busy with activities that they have come to see them as entitlements, and not privileges. This little girl will come to see that those fun activities come after they are earned with respectful, cooperative behavior.

Now let's talk about her younger brother. Because he is picked on constantly by his sister, he speaks in a voice one can barely hear, doesn't make eye contact, and whines like a baby.

I made the following recommendations to his dad: First, do not respond to whining. Second, do not respond when the child speaks in a barely audible voice.

I later got a text from the happy mother who said he behaved more self-confidently and had his first sleepover without incident.

DR. LAURA SAYS:

The moral of this story is that children have to earn their perks and parents are in charge. Few words, a strong attitude, and plenty of hugs go a long way.

Set a Good Example for Your Kids

A public service video on Australian television kicked up quite a storm when it blamed parents for the bad behavior of their children.

A mother is shown going up an escalator with her daughter. Both are smoking cigarettes. When they get to the top, the mother drops her cigarette and squishes it with her foot. Her child does the same. Then a father and son are shown finishing sodas and dropping the empty cans by the curb.

After that, the video-makers up the ante by showing a drunken mother stumbling down the street, grabbing the side of a building, and then throwing up. Her young daughter is shown doing the same.

So many times folks call my radio program complaining about the out-of-control behavior of their children. It is not unusual for me to ask the caller, "Which parent did your child learn this from?" It is quite astonishing when the caller sadly says, "Me."

42 is a terrific movie about Jackie Robinson, the first black major league baseball player. If you haven't seen it, it's available online to stream on a number of platforms. The most memorable scene is in the middle of the film. Jackie Robinson is up to bat. The white crowd goes wild with disgusting epithets and boos.

The camera settles on one father at the game with his about-eight-year-old son. The boy is beside himself with joy that he is going to see his hero, Brooklyn Dodger shortstop Pee Wee Reese, a teammate of Robinson.

However, the boy is stunned and upset to watch and hear his father screaming vile comments at Jackie Robinson. The boy looks around and sees all the other men in his seating area doing the same. It is clear he is trying to digest this situation. The little boy soon starts screaming ugly things along with his dad.

Pee Wee Reese then walks across the field to Robinson and simply puts his arm around Jackie's shoulder and smiles and chats. Pee Wee stands there, arm around Jackie, clearly showing fans that they are friends. The boy is confused. Whom should he follow? His dad? Pee Wee?

Tears well up in his eyes. He stops screaming with his dad.

There's a lot of karma to what your children see you say and do. Being a bad example will come back to bite you as well as damage your children. Good parents can have a badly behaved child. It happens. However, it is more likely that a child is difficult because of the example set by one or both parents.

DR. LAURA SAYS:

Your children are watching you for cues on how to be a good person.

Teens: Driven Crazy

Jim Rogenmoser, founder of Teen Driving Watch, emailed me because he was concerned about reducing teen driving accidents. He was wondering why so many parents, instead of protecting their children by signing them up for his program, say that by subscribing they think they are telling their new teen drivers that they don't trust them.

I hear that "worry" way, way too often from modern parents. When it comes to monitoring a teen's email and computer use, administering home drug tests, or paying close attention to their dating activities, parents will often take a pass, saying, "I don't want my son/daughter to think I don't trust them,"

What are those parents thinking? Of course you don't trust teenagers! Your teens:

- Have little life experience to fall back on when new circumstances and unforeseen challenges present themselves.
- Are naturally impulsive, which means they do whatever the moment suggests.
- Relax parental rules when their peers pressure them into being "their own person."
- Cannot really assess potential consequences (see bullet point 1) and have a sense of power and invincibility that belongs more in virtual games than real life.
- Would rather ask forgiveness than ask permission.
- Think that parental rules are over the top and controlling and not truly necessary.
- Tend to check limitations and push against them—like finding out if the car really can make that hairpin turn.
- Like speed and risk; they are excitement junkies.
- Need supervision to keep them on track, punctuated with controlled experiments in freedom to earn more.

The main problem we have in society today is that parents tend to be more involved in their own gratification and acquisition than in the sacrifices and difficulties necessary for appropriate parenting. With the high divorce rate with broken homes as well as the trend toward dual-career marriages, parents are both exhausted and appropriately guilty . . . which results in them spouting nonsense about kids' maturity and necessity for independence.

I don't believe for a moment that teenagers should own their own cars. First, it gives them a sense of autonomy, position, and power that they really haven't earned yet in life. Second, it gives children a feeling that they are adults because they have trans-portation affording them the privacy and freedom they crave—without the responsibility and maturity that should back that up.

So—now that you're thinking I'm totally nuts, remember that getting killed in car accidents is the number one way that teens die in America.

Parents have to be willing and able to stand up to teen pres-sure. Parents are responsible for protecting their children—even from themselves.

I believe children should have access to cars that the parents own, but if and only if they demonstrate enough self-control and respect for parental rules and property.

Passing driver's ed classes does nothing to guarantee a child's safety. It is necessary, but not sufficient.

And don't be afraid to pull the privilege away at the first sign of irresponsibility or breach of your rules. In fact, you might want to make a written contract that outlines what you expect and what will happen if those expectations, once accepted, are not respected. That way you minimize so-called misunderstandings. And if there are misunderstandings, remember that you are the parent and your perspective of the deal is the one that counts. You can change the deal if you think it appropriate—your child does not have equal power.

DR. LAURA SAYS:

I have long thought that making things too convenient for children does not help them in life. Having control of cars while having the word "teen" in describing their age doesn't give them much to look forward to in their adult life. Learning how to reach goals on their own, and paying all their expenses while learning to budget rather than having all adult perks as kids, is a better thing.

Booze Is Not for Kids, Period

Homecomings, proms, and graduations . . . booze, booze, and more booze. And, oh yes—drunken sex. But let's just focus on the alcohol for now.

There are actually parents who teach their children to "drink responsibly" by allowing them to consume alcohol under their supervision. They also host underage drinking parties thinking that children who consume alcohol while adults supervise will somehow become responsible about drinking. Wrong!

The lead author and a senior research associate at the school of nursing at the University of Minnesota conducted studies covering two continents and discovered that teens who drink with an adult supervising are more likely to develop problems with alcohol than kids who aren't allowed to drink until age 21.

I don't know why this surprises anybody. As with sex, parents need to make it clear that it's not okay for kids to drink until they reach the legal age. Parents need to point out their own mistakes and those of others who drank as children: not being able to stop drinking, getting violent and engaging in fights, getting injured or dying in car crashes, suffering serious hangovers, having sex with strangers, and being unable to remember anything that happened.

Teenagers are not smaller versions of adults. Their brains are not completely formed, and therefore the impact of alcohol is quite dramatic; long-term deficits in learning and memory are common results of repeated drinking.

Studies from the University of Pittsburgh Medical Center show that kids are four times more likely to become alcoholics if they start drinking before the age of 15.

Let me give you some more sobering statistics. Youths who drink alcohol are more likely to experience school problems, social problems (fighting and less participation in healthy activities), legal problems, physical problems, inappropriate sexual activity, disruption of normal growth and sexual development, physical and sexual assault, higher suicide and homicide risk, alcohol-related car crashes, burns, falls, drowning, memory problems, abuse of other drugs, changes in brain development that may have lifelong effects, and death from alcohol poisoning.

I hope that got your attention. It isn't cute for kids to get wasted—it is desperately destructive.

Although underage drinking is illegal, people aged 12 to 20 drink 11 percent of all alcohol consumed in the United States. On average, underage drinkers consume more drinks per drinking occasion than adult drinkers.

And while numbers are going down (likely due to expansion of Uber and other rideshare companies), teenage emergency room visits due to alcohol use are still over 100,000 each year.

Parents need to make sure that their children do not see them overdrinking, getting drunk, having parties where the participants get soused, and generally acting not very adultlike. That certainly is also not conducive to teaching children how to be responsible with alcohol.

DR. LAURA SAYS:

Alcohol is an adult beverage. Bottom line: Children should not drink until legal age when, the hope is, "moderation" has become their sacred mantra.

REFLECTIONS

Think for a moment about how important parenting is. You created new life and have the obligation and responsibility to help contribute a decent human being into the world. When you think about it that way, perhaps you can more appreciate how much your love, guidance, nurturance, and attention toward your children will impact the world!

CHAPTER EIGHT

Resilience

Bette Davis, an icon of the silver screen, is quoted as saying, "Old age ain't no place for sissies." Well, neither is life at any age. I even get calls from children as young as six asking me questions about how to handle nasty kids. Frankly, there are more nasty kids than ever. Why? Lousy or no parenting. When I was a kid, if I did anything wrong in the neighborhood, some parent called my parents and I was toast. That was the general attitude. No one took pride in a misbehaving child. These days, most kids are not even with their parents with divorce, remarriage, and two-career, very busy parents, day care, and so forth.

Busy parents don't want to know anything bad: annoying, time consuming, ego deflating. So . . . it is up to me to tell children how to do this themselves, because schools are afraid of lawyers and special interest groups and stupid rules that don't allow kids to protect themselves.

My mother told me never to hit others UNLESS they hit me first, and then I was to hit them back twice as hard. Ha!

But nowadays it is almost like *Lord of the Flies*, with unsupervised, underdisciplined kids with emotional issues due to busy parental neglect, using the Internet to raise the bar on humiliating and hurting other children.

Hell on earth.

Can Your Kid Handle a Bully?

Many stories about children who are being bullied with gossip begin in the same way.

The story commonly starts with a child telling a "friend" something very personal, and that friend tells others who tell others, and before you know it, everybody is giggling about whatever it is.

There also are kids who like to pick on others to feel superior, usually picking on a child who is not very assertive. Other kids, filled with envy about grades, looks, or possessions, take out their jealousy by trying to destroy that child's reputation.

And there are youngsters who are unhappy at home (because of neglect or some form of abuse or chaos with divorces, remarriage, and so forth), and they take their frustrations out on other kids.

Whatever the motivation, it hurts. It hurts you as the parent to see your child come home from school upset about schoolyard politics. It hurts your child, who feels trapped and helpless.

In my day, if you went to other parents and told them that their child was hurting yours, the other parents would apologize and call their kid on the carpet.

Today, I rarely recommend going to the other parents, because they tend to become hostile. That hostility further motivates the errant child, who feels "backed up" by defensive parents.

I often suggest, as a first response, for the child to just shrug it off and stay busy with another activity. If that doesn't work, we have to try other things.

For example: Have your child invite the annoying kid to your home for lunch, a game, or a movie. Befriending someone who is emotionally collapsed might just turn him or her into one of your child's biggest supporters and protectors!

If that doesn't work, teach your child to be more assertive. Those skills will be important for the rest of his or her life. Teach your child to speak up when the bully approaches—by describing out loud (without name-calling or insults) what is happening:

"You are going to call me bad names and try to make me feel bad? Okay ... go ahead ... I'm paying attention." When this is said in a loud voice so others can hear, it will provide the type of attention the bully doesn't want—making him or her feel awfully stupid.

If the bully gets physical, I believe that your child should know how to handle it. Some kickboxing lessons are good cardio and core training and invaluable in a situation where children have to protect themselves or someone else.

Ultimately, parents will have to teach children about the reality of bad people and that sometimes they will be at the receiving end of bad behavior and they will have to learn to deal with it.

You may want to tell stories from your childhood or work environment to illustrate that it can happen to anyone. Reinforce that just because somebody is out to get you doesn't make you worth less—it makes that person a creep.

Remind children that many other kids at school aren't doing anything unpleasant to them.

DR. LAURA SAYS:

Encourage children to spend more time with the good guys rather than worrying about the few bad guys.

Fight Back Against Bullying

Sorry folks, there is only one way to stop bullying ... but it will never happen. What I'm advocating is taking a stand—not a popular concept today.

Schools can have all the programs they can imagine in an attempt to teach children to "talk out their feelings," or "have options to rage reactions in annoying or frustrating situations," or "be nice," or whatever. None of that will ever work—not without supervision.

But if each and every time someone was bullied, everyone within sight would close in and threaten the bully, then bullying would stop quicker than overnight. But that will never happen. Why? Because most people are just not very caring or interested in the well-being of anyone other than themselves. Remember, I said most—not all.

When you look at the history of the world, you find innumerable examples of cataclysmic bullying, between countries and within countries. Remember Pol Pot of Cambodia and the "killing fields"? Everyone with an education was massacred along with their entire families. No one went in and stopped this carnage. Remember World War II and the German commitment to the "final solution" of eliminating all Jews? No one bombed the railways leading to the concentration camps. These are two of thousands of such examples.

Now, there are families and communities and specific religions that teach compassion. That's nice. But what is really important is families and communities and all religions teaching everyone to stand between evil and the innocent in spite of the potential consequences. That now is the height of being "human." During the Holocaust there were many Christians who risked their lives and the lives of their children to save Jews from annihilation. To this day, Israel honors them as "righteous gentiles." When any of these decent, brave human beings were asked why they did what they did, they did not consider themselves heroes. They all said one simple thing: "It was the right thing to do." Plain and simple.

I taught my son from an early age what my mother taught me at an early age: "Never hit anyone—unless they hit you or someone else. Then hit them twice as hard." Unfortunately, it is difficult to teach your children this credo in this era of ridiculous concepts that public schools revere: zero tolerance. Telling children not to physically protect themselves as well as others gives the bad guys all the power. It also teaches children to stand by when another child is being bullied, and that is disgustingly wrong.

These days children stand by cheering and taking videos to stream on the Internet. They mostly have the mentality of Romans watching Christians fed to lions or of gladiators fighting to the death as a means of entertainment. I don't see much difference between kids cheering and videoing and Romans cheering.

People must be taught to be good, brave, loyal, honest, and courageous. With our currently vicious society (check out college campuses and Congress), children have role models of creating havoc and chaos. With the high incidence of shacking up, hooking up, out-of-wedlock children, divorces with remarriages and more kids, and the anti-male feminist mentality, where can children learn the qualities they need in order to rise above being animals? Children today have few role models. *Heartbreak Ridge*, as horrendous a viewing experience as it was, is one of the very few movies to show true sacrificial heroism. Unfortunately one cannot take kids to that movie to witness the all-too-real carnage.

There are few television programs, video games, or movies that even think about—much less demonstrate—valor. Without these images, children cannot emulate the qualities that would stop bullies.

Clint Eastwood's character in *Grand Torino* starts out as a nasty old bigot. When Asians move in next door, and he befriends their bullied teenage boy, we see a man's man trying to help the boy become stronger while providing fatherly like protection. In the end, Eastwood's character sets up the bullying bad guys into shooting and killing him so they would finally be arrested and permanently off the street and out of the boy's life.

Granted, he was going to die of cancer soon; nonetheless with every day being precious, he gave that time up for the well-being of someone else.

These are two movies that put forth the notion of true hero-ism: putting yourself in harm's way for the benefit of another.

DR. LAURA SAYS:

Take every teenager you know to see *Grand Torino* and then discuss what should be everyone's moral obligation: to protect others.

How Bullying Victims Become Prey

Anti-bullying programs are springing up all over the country. They are well intentioned, yet most all of them miss an important point: how the "victim" has a role in becoming the "prey" to the bullies.

Over the years many parents have complained to me about their little one being picked on in school. One of the first things I ask is, "Why do you think your kid has a target on his (or her) back?"

After some defensive chatter, they usually cite behavior that makes their child stand out as an easy target. I suggest that their child needs to change certain behaviors. The parent is horrified to hear me supposedly "blaming the victim," but it isn't blame I'm after. It's an understanding of playground politics and the animal side of children.

Let me give a parallel. My Rhodesian ridgeback, Butch, is nine months old. He weighs more than 80 pounds, but he is still a baby and very much a wimp.

For him to be comfortable with his environment, he needs to be at ease with people, places, and things that make noise. When frightened, this big dog tries to jump into my arms.

I started taking him to off-leash parks and had numerous bad experiences: Dominant dogs would frighten him into running away or hiding behind me.

I asked the breeder what I could do, and he came up with a plan. The breeder brought several Ridgebacks to the park, and her husband brought five rescue dogs that he trains and rehabilitates.

A German shepherd and a pit bull challenged the heck out of Butch, and his lack of self-confidence stimulated more "animal" behavior from those dogs, meaning they got more aggressive toward him.

However, the shepherd and the pit bull were good with each other and the other dogs. Why? All these dogs were confident and experienced and knew how to handle the moment. Because of that, the more aggressive animals did not see them as prey.

So Butch is working through his insecurities and becoming more confident and experienced handling "playground politics."

While it is true that some kids will pick on others for something that can't be changed, such as physical attributes, many children who bully—or go along with the bullies—also look for weakness.

That's why I tell parents to enroll their kids in martial arts; not to fight (unless necessary), but to develop a sense of strength, pride, and confidence. They will then walk, talk, and handle situations with more strength and look less like a target.

Help your children develop an aura of confidence, a sense of humor, tactics for working with playground politics, and ultimately other strategies to protect themselves if things get physical. I often even suggest that the picked-on kid invite the bully for a day of play and lunch, which throws the bully way off!

DR. LAURA SAYS:

Most "monster" kids will respond well to kindness—which is what most of them are missing in their lives anyway.

How Families Cope with Disaster

Unfortunately, dreadful and terrible events happen to us all. Some are natural disasters, some are merely accidents, and some are a part of life. And while death, loss, and injury are horrendous experiences to have to deal with, psychologically we are somewhat more philosophical about encounters with horror that aren't "personal."

The horrors that are personal include the evil that people intentionally do to cause harm to body, soul, property, psychological well-being, and the reputation of another for political gain or financial gain. Or to stroke their own egos—or for the simple pleasure derived from having the power to destroy. These experiences turn out to be more difficult to cope with because they are not seen as "stuff that could happen to anyone."

Also, there is great compassion and sympathy for those struck by nature, while personal attacks on an innocent party are generally ignored by onlookers who have a profound fear of helping, lest one get caught in the sights of the evildoer. Therefore, the support necessary is often less in size and strength—which adds insult to injury for the already damaged person.

The evolution of talk radio and television news from information to confrontation, as well as the loss of any ethical foundation for the print and online media—especially the unleashing of anonymous venom on the Internet and social media—not only has served to destroy reputations with undocumented vicious gossip, but has lowered the level of discourse and civility to an unbelievably dangerous level.

Decent folks who wish to serve their country in the military, politics, social work, and other public arenas become fodder for indecent attacks based upon ideology, with the sole purpose of eliminating their voices and ability to function.

Gone is the civility of negotiation, arbitration, discussion, and debate.

Soon, only the indecent will reign. Our enemies have only to wait: We are destroying our own society.

Our American society is becoming alarmingly ugly and dangerous.

How can a family and its members survive? It is difficult— and sometimes barely possible.

When bad things happen, the first reaction of most family members is a kind of "shock," in which people seem not to be that upset—it is more disbelief or a sense of incomprehension. Once the truth and reality become tangible, that's when the pain, grief, hurt, fear, and anxiety set in. If the situation appears hopeless, and the people involved feel helpless to protect themselves or their loved ones, a horrible depression infiltrates every bone of their bodies.

This is a critical time for a family. It is at this time that intervention by meaningful intimates is absolutely crucial. It is at this terrible time that people often contemplate direct or indirect suicide: driving a car over a cliff or overdosing with some dangerous medication.

Family members might turn against each other, imagining that they alone are really feeling the pain and that the others don't really understand and can't help. When the enemy is nature or an evildoer, it is often difficult or impossible to get revenge or justice. That concern alone sometimes leaves people lashing out where they can: on family.

What most folks truly need at a time like this is threefold:

1. Families need to provide each other with complete support and expression of understanding for the magnitude of the painful situation. That means you don't placate, minimize, patronize, try to distract with cheerful activities, or attempt to whitewash with perspective by saying things like, "There is worse happening out there in the world."

    Instead, you need to hug and acknowledge that this is indeed awful, and they are justified to be feeling every horrible feeling they're going through. When, for example, people call my radio program telling me of their emotional state in reaction to some horrible assault, I tell them, "That is a reasonable response to an unreasonable situation." In other words, you validate the truthfulness of their perception and response. You must validate the truth of a family member's reality, or you run the risk of making the person feel more "crazy."

2. You must make sure the members of your family eat properly to avoid headaches and depression. You must get sleep, even if it means temporarily using sleep medications (over-the-counter types if at all possible). And depending on their level of despair, make sure you watch each other in case a temporary despondency might lead to their hurting themselves.

3. Get advice for a game plan that deals with the situation. This gives family members hope and relieves some of the helplessness. This stage is usually associated with anger,

which has to be controlled and focused in a positive direction—one that will not add to the problem, but will ultimately approach justice.

DR. LAURA SAYS:

Our society has become a meaner, harsher, and more dangerous place than ever before. I don't know what can turn it back. I mourn for the America that was the safe haven of the world.

How to Learn from Losing

A seemingly small question from a caller; a dramatically larger question for American society: "How can I teach my six-year-old son to be a good loser?"

Good question, America.

Here was my answer:

1. **Role-modeling.** When children are brought up in a home atmosphere where triumph and defeat are both met with equanimity, the child learns both not to gloat and not to rage. Parents often don't realize how they themselves become short, critical, frustrated, angry, or petty and pouty when things don't go their way either at work or at play. Children watch; children learn. It is often surprising how many parents see the flaw of bad sportsmanship, impatience, and self-hating rage in their child, but not in the mirror.

2. **Giving positive feedback.** When positive reinforcement of children's efforts, much less their whole being, seems to be contingent upon winning or being the best, the children

are threatened down to their core when they don't do well at something. They feel that they've let their parents down and also that their worth and lovability is a function of winning—which becomes an "at all costs" issue because those children are fighting for the value of their life. Parents need to separate out their children's worth from specific accomplishments and always find something to laud about their efforts.

3. **Instilling values.** When I was growing up, I read many short stories and books about "good sportsmanship." These stories were clear about right and wrong, with wrong including cheating, interfering with someone else's efforts to succeed, refusing to admit defeat, and being mean to others because of the loss. These vivid lessons reinforce in children that the quality of a human being and of relationships is more important than the results of any competition. These lessons did not imply that winning had no meaning—quite the contrary. These stories supported the notion of hard work, perseverance, and goal orientation. But they were clear that ultimately the quality of life comes from character, not from a trophy.

4. **Controlling feelings.** Feelings have become elevated to the sacred in our society. If people are offended, uncomfortable, sad, fearful, and so forth, they seem to think they have a "license to kill" (figuratively speaking, of course).

     Children need to know that simply because they feel sad or bad, they don't have to, nor should they permit themselves to, unleash those feelings in the form of angry, hysterical, or vengeful behaviors. Children must learn to sublimate normal feelings and continue to motivate the direction of their behaviors by their values of self-discipline, sensitivity, and compassion toward others.

Too many parents, especially moms, try to make the hurt go away by any means . . . even by misguiding or spoiling their children. It is far better to let children feel these human reactions and learn to control their acting out; it is a more painful but more mature route.

5. **Applauding the winner.** Children should be taught that upon the completion of a competition that does not go in their favor, they should immediately congratulate the winner. They should also be taught to point out the qualities or actions of their successful opponent that led to the win! This gracious behavior feeds back into a more positive mood and attitude of the "nonwinner."

6. **Learning.** Children should be taught to study the competition and learn from it. They need to look at their own actions to decide whether more training, experience, practice, focus, technique, etc., would be helpful for their future. They should use every experience to learn how to grow and improve. They should be made to understand that competition is a journey and that each instance is but a step.

7. **Teaching.** Children should be supported to share their level of competency with those behind them. This responsibility teaches patience and respect for the learning process. It also has children learning compassion.

DR. LAURA SAYS:

When children are appreciated and supported for their strengths, they tend to be willing to face life with more courage and compassion.

REFLECTIONS

One of the most important gifts you give your children (and indirectly yourself!) is the knowledge that you love them and will support them through their struggles BUT you will NOT support them through their ill-doing; for that, they will have to suffer consequences.

It doesn't help your kids when you lovingly bring cookies to them in prison.

Part Three

FAMILY, FRIENDS, & RELATIONSHIPS

Life is short (I just made that up, right?),
and it's important that you fill it with blessings.

Having quality relationships depends upon your having standards for what you will accept, upholding standards yourself, and demonstrating kindness and compassion, but definitely not supporting behavior that hurts others.

Relationships have uptimes and downtimes, and speaking openly and truthfully, as scary and uncomfortable as that might be, is an absolute necessity. Without open communication, nobody really knows what is going on inside another, and that opens the door for misunderstandings and situations from which there is no return.

Whether with family or friends, take care . . . take care.

CHAPTER NINE

Reality Check for Relationships

I frankly have never understood cafés that actually cater to individuals who hog a table for hours while they play on their laptops or cell phones or read on their Kindles. For me, walking into a café, seeing these folks buried in cyberspace, is a real turn-off, and I turn and leave.

I guess many café owners and managers believe that, without these squatters, they wouldn't have business. Many people believe that if you can't fight 'em, you've got to cater to them.

Not so. There are some courageous cafés that are banning laptops and cell phones. Besides smelling the coffee, you hear the sound of people actually chatting with one another—with friends, with coworkers, with family—building and strengthening relationships.

In the late afternoons, people are writing on actual paper, reading print newspapers, and lingering over books in a corner. The manager makes the rounds, talking to solo folks. Person-to-person contact is valued. Humanity is resurrected. Resistance isn't futile.

I would like to challenge everyone to spend a day without any electronic connections attached. Humans are gregarious creatures; we yearn for contact. See whether you make more meaningful, satisfying contacts face-to-face than hooking yourself up to the electronic universe. Reach out and actually touch somebody.

How to Say I'm Sorry

"I'm sorry" is probably not said enough, and when it is said, it is too often not sincerely offered. Many times it is offered to just shut down the problem or argument or is said in a condescending manner.

Yet it remains one of the most important exchanges between people. If said properly, it is the magic that repairs rifts in relationships and families.

"I'm sorry," all by itself, has little impact. In order to be effective and repair the damage and hurt feelings, it has to be specified and personalized. In order to be taken seriously, the "I'm sorry" must be attached to two very important facts: It has to specify who was hurt and what the hurtful aspect was.

Here's an example: "I'm sorry that I upset you by sharing your secret with somebody else." In this declaration you are not hedging or being defensive. You are using a declarative sentence to point out exactly what you did that was wrong. You're aware and taking responsibility.

Additionally, by specifying "you," you are removing any confusion or generalization about the action.

When we put those two elements together with the "sorry," any possible need for argument or defensive actions is minimized.

And here is where you have to be careful not to mess up the good you've done so far. Never add a "but" or attempt to minimize your responsibility with excuses. Excuses should never be offered. They dilute the apology and start the hurt all over again.

It is insincere to apologize with, "If I did something that upset you," or "Whatever it was that got you angry," or any other halfway apologies. These words minimize what you've done as well as show disrespect for what the person suffered at your hand.

I have been in situations where I said or did something that unintentionally hurt someone. Although the intent wasn't there, the pain is just the same. The apology stays, but it is important to add something like, "Please believe me when I say I did not intend to hurt you. Intent or not, I did hurt you, and I am sorry for . . ."

And then follow up.

DR. LAURA SAYS:

Ask what you might do to repair the damage or make amends. This should be a dialogue. The more the conversation goes back and forth, the better result you will both have in apologizing and being forgiven.

Decent, Honest People Have Become Rare Treasures

It strikes me how surprised we all are these days when someone acts like a decent, honest human being.

What sparked my interest in writing about this is a story I saw about a man at the busy Las Vegas McCarran International Airport who found some envelopes on the ground. When he picked them up and felt them, it was clear to him that the envelopes were filled with cash. He didn't open them to see how much. He just stood there holding the envelopes in plain sight for over half an hour, waiting for someone to come and retrieve them.

Our man went home and called the airport from time to time to ask if anyone inquired about the envelopes. Finally, the answer was yes. He still held onto the envelopes until he got confirmation from the owner about how much money was in the envelopes. When he heard the correct answer ($10,000!), he returned the money and refused a reward.

What was amazing about this story was his admission that many friends and family told him that he was crazy to return the money. They were stunned that he would do so.

When he was interviewed on television, he was asked about the temptation to keep the cash. He smiled, shrugged, and said that he wanted to show his children the right thing to do.

As another example, a young man we know recently came over to our home and told us he had just come across a car on a lonely stretch of road that had its emergency lights blinking. Without giving it a second thought, he stopped and asked the driver if he needed any help. The driver was ecstatic, exclaiming that he'd called AAA over an hour ago and no help had come. Cars passed without anyone even slowing down to see what problem he might be having.

Our young friend asked him what he could do to help, and the man asked for a lift into town. During that short drive the man offered him some money to thank him for helping. He said, "Absolutely not. Glad to help."

The young man drove to our home, and when he parked, he noticed a $100 bill on his dash. Looks like this gentleman wouldn't take no for an answer.

This fellow is military. Honor and service are built into the training and the man. Many of you reading this probably have such uplifting stories of your own.

A woman found my wedding ring on the floor of the dry cleaners we use (silly me—must have put it in a pocket) and returned it to us and refused a reward in spite of being a single mom with a very modest income. I had her and her daughter visit my radio show and prepared a basket of goodies for her little girl.

What is sad is that when most of us tell such stories of someone being so honest and totally lacking greed, we are surprised. Our national role models have been so very disappointing: Government waste, corporate wrongdoing, illegal investments, cheating, and stealing seem to be the norm in our culture.

"Finders keepers; losers weepers" seems to have become our motto.

We need to resist that message and look for opportunities to help someone else.

DR. LAURA SAYS:

I've seen that all humanity can be improved by a simple act of kindness and honesty.

Know Your Limitations

It is way too easy to get overwhelmed—even by elements in your life you enjoy: family, work, hobbies, community involvement, and even yoga, etc. We tend to often underestimate the impact of multiple investments of our emotion, time, effort, concentration, and energy.

Contrary to anything you've been taught or may have heard, human beings do have limits! You definitely cannot give 100 percent to multiple venues without an impending crash. Crashes take on many forms: feeling tired, sad, or impatient; even anger pop ups.

The main problem I have experienced with people coming to me for help is that they simply don't want to admit they are overwhelmed and/or burned out. They seem to see this as a sign of some kind of weakness and feel somewhere between ashamed and frustrated. They simply WANT to be able to do everything. That passion comes from a fear of feeling undervalued to others if they can't pull it off. And it is true that those in each of your many domains may indeed get annoyed if you don't give them all that they are expecting and you promised. That is absolutely true! They have the right to feel somewhat let down because in their mini-universe, things just have to get done and get done now and correctly. So that fear is right on!

It appears that people dread—absolutely dread—the notion of listing priorities, making choices, and taking things off their plate. Ouch! To so many it feels like abject failure. I believe it is a failure to not acknowledge limits, as in the famous words of Dirty Harry, "A (wo)man has to know her/his limitations." And we all have them. Not because we are damaged, incompetent, or stupid; but simply because we are human. As such, 100 percent is all each of us has, not multiples of such. That means that you actually have to make choices after listing your priorities. If you have small children, their welfare is number one, which has always meant to me that you need to find a way to work even your job around their needs, for them to be parented hands-on by mommy and/or daddy.

The way I help people make decisions on my daily radio program (you can hear it on SiriusXM 111) is to almost literally force them to tell me what is the most important issue in their lives. Believe you me, it becomes easier to make deletions and alterations once you acknowledge what is the center point of your concern.

If it is to be involved with extended family, then you shouldn't go off with someone you just met on the Internet some 1,000 miles away from home base—no matter how great a fantasy it all seems to be. If you want to take that big job risk, first comes the security of your family—then you organize what you have to do.

People with conscience and character have an easier time with this than those who are immature or narcissistic; these conditions lead to more of a sense of entitlement and impulsiveness, which usually leads people to get overwhelmed by losses caused by their poor decisions as well as the disappointment of fantasies not being met.

Being overwhelmed means cutting back, making choices, and dividing up that 100 percent in the most productive and honorable way. It does not mean getting some "booty" on the side or indulging in alcohol, drugs, porn, gambling, and so forth to medicate the confusion and frustration.

DR. LAURA SAYS:

It's all about priorities.

Everyone Can be Happy

Feeling hopeless leads to diminished motivation and depression. In the 1960s psychologists did experiments with monkeys. They had them in cages made of metal, through which they administered an abrupt electric shock (torture is the correct term). The animals tried valiantly to escape the shock . . . and when they couldn't, they simply became passive, almost catatonic. The same sort of thing happens to people on an emotional level. If you experience considerable frustrations, aggravations, disappointments, and defeats, hopelessness sets in and depression follows.

When you don't have hope, you're not motivated to make any effort. Why bother? It's all going to be crappy anyway. That attitude becomes self-fulfilling. If you don't put in any effort, nothing positive can happen. This email from Sarah is important when considering how one might more positively respond to depressive feelings:

> Hi, Dr. Laura. I just wanted to share something that came to mind tonight while I was kneeling in my closet, crying. I suffer from some postpartum depression and anxiety. I had no particular reason to be miserable. I came to a realization: I was, in that moment, not happy. But I knew that I could be again. And that's good enough. I decided that I'm going to start making more good choices that lead to happiness: getting to bed on a regular schedule, taking care of my body and mind, etc. I may not be happy now, but I can be, and I will be. With hope, a happy mom, Sarah

She decided on hope. Remarkable. Curled up in a ball in her closet crying, and she chose hope. Sarah is my hero.

I was talking to a person the other day who had a lot of reasons to be very sad. I manipulated her into using the word "sad" rather than "depressed" because the sad word doesn't have the ugly finality to it that the depressed word has, so saying to yourself that you feel "sad" feels less hopeless and less aggravating to the state of mind.

I said to her, "Today when you go to that event, put on a cute dress and some makeup."

"Why?" she asked.

"Because when we put on a cute dress and makeup, we feel better. When you catch your reflection, you will be lifted by the image of you not looking as bad as you feel. Also, when you get up tomorrow, make yourself a nice breakfast."

"Why?" she asked again.

"Because when you get up and eat a nice breakfast, it makes you feel better; and having food in your tummy and sugar levels in your bloodstream, you feel better." She did both, and she did feel better.

These small things make a difference. Small things can make you feel better. Talking the situation through with kind people who are supportive and can help you solve some of the problems dragging you down is essential. Being honest with yourself about what you truly want to do in your life (rather than pleasing others as your main focus) is essential.

I have spoken to many young adults who are not on their own path, but on the path their parents expect. They become hopeless and depressed. Many of these parents are well meaning, thinking that college and a specialty will give their child the best in life.

One mother argued with me when I told her to back down as she was forcing her daughter into a four-year college program when her daughter wanted, with a passion, to do hair and makeup. The mother was disrespectful of that as a career. I understood that girl's feelings—my father disrespected psychology as a career!

In the past year we have read about a number of very successful folks committing suicide. As I tried to read between the lines to find a pattern, I basically came up with the understanding that folks ferociously driven by money, success, and celebrity literally run themselves into the ground. We see massive drug and alcohol abuse, multiple marriages, schedules that could drop anyone to the ground. And used in a different sense, "ground" is the operative word here. People who do the best in life are grounded in family, friends, pleasant activities, travel for relaxation . . . they are grounded in life instead of being a gerbil trapped in a cage, running the cylindrical exerciser going nowhere.

Studies also demonstrate that folks who do things for others increase their serotonin levels (the happy chemical of the brain).

In other words, instead of an inward focus on how screwed up everything is for you, reaching out to someone else thwarts feelings of hopelessness and depression.

DR. LAURA SAYS:

We can't expect to be happy all the time. Sarah's point is well taken: We can be happy again.

REFLECTIONS

It's logical to try to regain control when it is clear that you really don't have any over circumstances that are ripping out your heart. I'm convinced that certain accidental medicinal overdoses and car accidents are the result of people feeling so imposed upon by ugly fate that they turn their pain and rage inward in a desperate attempt to feel less like a helpless victim.

If you know someone in this condition, please don't try to use logic ("Things will change—they always do") or guilt ("You have so much—how dare you not appreciate your blessings"). These techniques only add to the pain. They get you no closer to a sense of understanding, a sense that you realize that person's world is imploding.

The best thing to do for people in this place is to make gentle physical contact (as in petting their head or arm or leg), bring them tea or coffee, and acknowledge the truth: They have been treated very unfairly. Tell them they're right, and it is outrageous. And then just be there quietly.

Many people are afraid to acknowledge the reality because they worry that the truth will just make it worse. It doesn't. The truth relieves the suffering individuals of the necessity to argue to try to get you to understand what they're going through. Arguing escalates their desperately black feelings, not the truth!

Don't ask a lot of questions about details. Just agree that the situation right now is bad. Just be there.

Consider one's life like a basket, filled with eggs of activities, hopes, desires, trusted people, etc. When one of these eggs breaks, it oozes all over all the other valued eggs and seeps through the reeds of the basket. It is never useful simply to point out all the other eggs; they've been gooped up, too. That's how the depressed person sees it.

Ultimately, you might suggest cleaning off the other eggs, transferring some out of the basket, and letting new ones in. Life works better when you "mix it up." Balance is never truly "restored"—balance eventually is re-created out of myriad different components. Give that person (or yourself) time to get to that place.

CHAPTER TEN

Dealing with Conflict

It is a really bad idea to harbor anger and resentment for years on end and never have the air cleared at the time of the cause of bad feelings. Most of the time issues can be relatively easily resolved because there was a simple misunderstanding. But if you never ask, you will never know, and you will just let the monster build in your head. Families are too often torn apart by such behaviors. Sometimes it isn't a misunderstanding—you were righteously wronged! Nonetheless, never let feelings fester, because your growing unhappiness poisons you as well as those who love you.

Deal with Family Conflicts BEFORE Holiday Gatherings

Whenever it gets close to holiday time, I am deluged with callers to my radio program desperate for advice on how to handle rude, insulting spouses; family members they accuse of molestation; in-laws who are boorish, self-centered, critical, and argumentative; relatives with out-of-control children; relatives who are on drugs; relatives who have abandoned their children and spouses for a "bimbo" and said bimbo wants to come to the holiday dinner . . . and the list goes on.

First of all, please don't deal with these issues at the event. It is rude and unfair to others to have confrontations during a party, dinner, or get-together. Your concerns should be dealt with way in advance of the event, and a decision needs to be made between attending or not. If you decide to attend, the commitment must be made to simply "be polite."

People often get themselves all tied in knots and anguished trying to figure out how they can accomplish everything on their wish list. They want to take a stand, but are afraid of the kickback. They are furious that someone has invited someone who they feel should not be invited—and perhaps should be ostracized. They want justice, retribution, revenge, and/or payback. They want someone, anyone, to choose them over the "bad" person.

Brace yourself for the reality that way too many people just keep on keeping on despite the blatantly unacceptable or even evil behavior that they invited into their midst. The biggest problem with evil is that—as the saying goes—good people stand by and do nothing. Well, the problem I've always had with that saying is that I believe that good people never stand by and do nothing. What they do in the face of evil defines them as good or not. It is easier to appear to be good when not challenged than to choose between darkness and light.

And it doesn't matter if the egregious act happened personally to you. Frankly, I admire people who stand up for others. I would never, ever accept an invitation to any event, family or otherwise, in which, for example, a known family molester was appearing. I would not bring my minor children to an event where a family member was showing off a swollen belly with no wedding ring . . . that hurts my children's developing sense of what is right and wrong (and intentionally robbing a child of a parent and a foundation of a traditional family is self-centered at best).

So here is what I want you to do. Call your mother, aunt, grandmother, sister, or whoever is hosting the event and discuss your issue in advance. If you come to realize that your attendance is much less important (even to your own mother) than "the destructive or dangerous" individual, politely offer that you won't be attending, and that you're disappointed these issues are being ignored for the sake of "fake" family unity, not being "judgmental," or having nobody be mad at them.

DR. LAURA SAYS:

Don't fight—just explain. You can always visit on another occasion when you are in control of the guest list.

Don't Forgive, Don't Forget—but Let Go

Years ago, someone I trusted took advantage of me in a big way.

It is not the only time it has happened to me. It is a fact of life that there are folks out there willing to manipulate others for personal gain.

Years later I walked up to him in a public arena and asked him if I could talk to him. First, I told him in no uncertain terms what he had done. Then I told him I was sad and angry about it because the relationship we had up to that point had been so mutually satisfying and beneficial that I missed that.

When I was done, I expected him to walk away. Instead he looked me square in the eye and said, "I did a lot of things wrong, and I have regret."

I was quite surprised. I thanked him for handling the moment the way he did. He then asked—surprise again—if he could hug me. I decided it was fine, as a public demonstration of his remorse. We are now quite pleasant to each other.

The other day a third party commented that it was nice that I forgave him. My response was: "No, I haven't forgiven him. I just decided to let it go."

So many people get "letting it go" and "forgiveness" confused. And since "forgiveness" has a profound religious connotation for some people, they almost feel obligated to use that word when indeed in their hearts they can't or shouldn't forgive.

Yes, there are some things that I believe are unforgivable.

"I'm sorry I murdered your child" or "I'm sorry I molested you your whole childhood" does not earn forgiveness in my book. But it does ease the rage somewhat, even if said only to avoid punishment. It is hard to know someone's soul.

After an offense occurs, I recommend always to let some time go by so both parties can think about what has happened. It is important for people to confront the wrongdoer and present the facts about the injury without demanding an apology. If after presenting your point of view the other person does not deal with you in an honorable way, it's time to walk away. If full responsibility is admitted and responsibility is taken, it is possible for you to unburden your psyche and just let it go. It is a good feeling to have your hurt recognized, acknowledged, and respected.

DR. LAURA SAYS:

"Letting it go" is to give up hating. One can be safe in the knowledge that you "know who they are" and you have survived the hurts they inflicted on you.

Don't Let Misunderstanding Ruin Friendship

For a span of over four decades, three or four hours a day, five days a week, I have listened on my radio show to people struggling with inner, and sometimes outer, demons. I have also listened to how the combination of tender feelings and misunderstandings can destroy perfectly good relationships.

My example will be a seemingly simple situation: Two women have been friends for some 20 years. One of them is having a birthday. Generally, on their birthdays one takes the other out for lunch, shopping, and general girl bonding.

This year my caller, the one without the birthday, is planning to attend a family event out of town and won't be able to be there on her friend's birthday. So she calls her friend and tells her that she'll take her out for their yearly celebration on another day. So far, so good.

Well, it turns out the birthday girl is planning a party this year on her birthday. The day before, the caller reminds her she will be out of town and won't be able to make it to the party. However, after a long conversation about so many little things, the caller, without thinking, makes a mistake and says, "See you tomorrow," as she hangs up. It goes straight to hell from there.

The caller does go to the family event, missing the birthday party. Her friend later leaves her a furious voice message about not showing up. The caller complains that her friend is a pouty princess whom she had informed she would be out of town and would celebrate another day.

I asked the caller to call her friend and find out what has made her so angry.

She calls me back the next day to tell me about their conversation. This is the first time I hear that she had said, "See you tomorrow," before hanging up with her friend. My caller is still on her angry high horse.

Now the whole thing is clear to me: It's a classic case of tender feelings and a misunderstanding threatening a friendship.

I told the caller:

You don't get the main point here! Your friend really, really likes you, and it meant a lot to her to have you, her dear friend, at her party. Not having you there was a real disappointment. When you said, 'See you tomorrow,' you said it as simply a parting phrase. She took it as you having made the decision to be at the party.

It is not an insult that she is hurt; it is a compliment. Now call her back and say, "Sorry," and then kiss and make up. Don't lose a perfectly good relationship this way. Please.

This sort of thing happens all the time between friends, spouses, and even coworkers. Simple misunderstandings of what someone said or meant turn into so much more. Not a person alive has ever avoided such circumstances. That is why it is so important to put on the brakes before reacting when you are surprised and hurt by something you think someone meant.

People use words and phrases incorrectly and sometimes without much thought to their potential impact.

That is why communication is so important—ask!

More often than not you will probably hear something different from what you presumed was said or meant—and then instead of losing a friend, you'll both have something to laugh about.

DR. LAURA SAYS:

Communicate before your blood pressure starts to rise!

Happiness—the Best Revenge for Betrayal

Betrayal seems to be a universal and eternal reality of the nature of human beings. We barely get into Genesis when one brother, in a fit of sibling rivalry over a perception of God's favor, kills the other brother.

Biblical human history starts with Eve betraying God and suckering Adam into a bite of forbidden fruit. Adam then betrays Eve by throwing her under the bus, making her take responsibility for his action in munching what he shouldn't.

Whether or not you look at biblical writings as history or metaphor, we are left with the same conclusion: Betrayal seems to be an inevitable, vicious, devastating, horrific part of the human condition.

One male listener of my radio program confided about being betrayed by his now ex-wife, who tried to turn their child and all their friends and relatives against him as a smokescreen that barely hid the multiple affairs she'd been having with coworkers.

Instead of blowing a gasket or getting outta Dodge, he put on a smiley face. His revenge was to be the kind of man and father that his ex would regret not having and that his daughter would adore. "Then I come home, my daughter comes running, yelling, 'Daddy, my daddy!' as loudly as she can. My ex-wife still holds the anger of her own mistakes and is living with shack-up number three since the divorce. My daughter knows the chaos in her mother's shack-up world and spends no less than five to six days a week with me."

Daddy transferred his rage at his ex-wife into love for his daughter and has sacrificed his personal and sex life to focus on her needs and security. Sublimation of ugly feelings into benevolent action is like using trash for fertilizer instead of an assault.

When people are out to get you, they delight in knowing they forced you into a corner or totally out the door. That's the worst thing for you to let them see, especially when they are but one rotten element in an otherwise okay situation. Even before you feel strong enough to do so, straighten up, throw your shoulders back, put a smile on your face, and start attending events you've been avoiding out of hurt or misplaced embarrassment with your head held high and your smile turned on maximum. This will jump-start your growth in self-confidence, and your increased strength will help you take on all kinds of new experiences because you'll learn to trust your own ability to survive.

DR. LAURA SAYS:

As one listener put it, "I guess my revenge was to be beautiful inside and out and let them eat their hearts out that they can't touch me!"

In Long-Term Relationships, Accept What You Cannot Change

I've noticed a disturbing increase lately in people who want some situation—usually in their personal relationships—to be other than what it is.

I will admit that commitment to a cause is admirable, but when stubbornness leads to the inability to face reality, it is not admirable. It is masochistic, and people hurt only themselves. It is not a positive move in a healthy direction.

This is true with lovers, spouses, relatives, and even parents. I am stunned at how often folks will allow a clearly manipulative, destructive, or parasitic parent to wreak havoc on their marriage and family.

I hear the excuses daily: "But it is my mother." "But I feel guilty." "But . . . but . . . but."

The truth is that even though these people are married with children, they simply haven't given up the lost cause of having a normal, warm, loving relationship with someone (their parent) who is almost entirely incapable of doing so.

They give up time, space in their home, emotion, attention, and their own well-being to that parent while their spouse and children suffer. It is entirely a selfish attempt to rewrite the past rather than accept the present as a truer measure of lovability.

Children who were neglected or abandoned by a parent, or, for whatever reason, had a bad relationship with a parent, believe they must be lacking in some way. It can create an eternal struggle to get love from that parent and can take up most of their heart, emotion, and mind—no matter how old or how accomplished they are or how others love them in the present. And this is tragic.

Those adult children of unloving parents must accept that the parent is incapable of love and that the past cannot be rewritten. They must learn that the lack of love from that parent is in no way a true measure of their worth.

Those who love you now know you best. Check out my book *Bad Childhood–Good Life: How to Blossom and Thrive in Spite of an Unhappy Childhood*. It will help you come to terms with your past, deal with your resentment, and allow healthy love into your life in the present.

DR. LAURA SAYS:

When you begin to accept what cannot change and stand up for yourself, you will begin to see your life have more depth and meaning.

REFLECTIONS

It is of course very difficult to give up on your fantasies and wishes for a perfect relationship with a parent. Some people just never stop trying to engage and hope that a miracle will occur. Sadly, I so often have to get these callers, who often are hanging on way into their middle age, hoping and trying to turn mother into a mommy and father into a daddy, to say: "I never had a mommy/daddy, I don't have a mommy/daddy, and never will have a mommy/daddy." I remind them to turn to the people who do love and care for them rather than continuing begging, suffering repetitive disappointments and slights.

CHAPTER ELEVEN

Dealing with Loss and Disappointment

Life is truthfully a series of challenges to your equanimity, happiness, and survival both physically and emotionally. Sometimes people in the middle of a painful situation think that they are the only ones. "Why me?" is what is generally said.

Everybody on the face of the earth has "Why me" circumstances . . . annoying but true. People are not happy because things always go well. People are happy because they accept reality with courage, work to make the best of things, and are grateful for the sunny times . . . which, by the way, still exist in the midst of misery. The sun is still shining when clouds cloak it.

The Best Way to Cope with Grief or Loss

Don't think you are alone if you have trouble getting over the loss of a friend, a job, your ability, or a family member. Death is not the only way we lose people. We can lose them through misunderstandings, egregious behavior, or even downright stupidity. The cause of the loss sometimes does matter because some things can possibly be repaired, while other circumstances yield situations that are untenable.

For example, texting is a brief way to communicate—but a shorthand form of communication about issues that are meaningful or touchy is a recipe for disaster. Misunderstandings that annoy, seem like insults, or appear to be insensitive or outright flippant can breach a trust between people very easily.

People write things in haste—things they might never say face-to-face or even on a phone call. These situations can often be repaired with direct communication complete with apology and explanation of what was truly intended. I am not even including situations wherein younger folks (or anyone else for that matter) text something mean or secret and hit Send to the wrong person. When that happens, the target becomes aware of backstabbing. I don't think that is typically fixable.

We are each in our own worlds. I remember my mother telling me that when she was a teenager in Italy, her mother died. She was devastated. She stood by her bedroom window and looked out at the busy street and was shocked to see people going about their business: walking, talking, laughing, biking, eating. She remembered wondering how everything could just go on for everyone else while her life had just been punched in the gut. It is an image I have never gotten out of my head. As much as my pain or happiness is, it is a mere speck in the universe.

We have to respect that, in relationships, people in our lives are not just in our lives; they are in their own lives first. Therefore, it takes effort to see beyond our own nebula and attempt to reconcile the coexisting goals, needs, expectations, abilities, and intentions someone may have.

Of course, we can't do that on an ongoing basis because we are immersed in our own realities. This is where compassion, sympathy, and an attempt to understand the other person's point of view are essential. One of the most rewarding and typical experiences I have on my radio program is when a caller lays out a feeling of anger or hurt and I can find a way to provide perspective about how it looks from the other person's point of view.

With women calling about day care and saying it is "just fine" because "everyone is doing it" and they just can't be without their jobs, I give them the child's point of view: a whole day without love. To the men who call and tell me that they have minor children from a divorce and are ready to marry a woman who wants to produce her own children, I say, "Nice . . . so your kids get to visit a dad raising some other woman's children full-time. How would that feel to you?"

All relationships need you to see the other side. Pretend you are the defense attorney for the other side (friend, spouse, coworker). How would you make that person's point? It is a great exercise in caring about someone else. Caring about someone else does not only mean you be polite to that person—it means that you try to see that person's situation.

When all doesn't go well and we lose someone who has mattered, there is no quick fix. Losing a part of life or limb takes adjustment and learning to endure pain as you try to find plan B to get on with your life. Talking to friends is important; just don't overwhelm them.

Getting physically active is a great idea, because between distraction and endorphins you will feel energized. Getting involved in new activities is wonderful, because it feels like growth and life. If all fails, that's when therapy might be useful.

DR. LAURA SAYS:

Not going over the situation again and again and again is important—just enough analysis to learn something important from what happened so you are better prepared to cope with and confront situations in the future.

Time for Regret, Not Guilt

One Saturday afternoon, I caught an episode of Rod Serling's *The Twilight Zone*. In its day, it was a significant series, because it dealt with important issues while also being creepy and thrilling.

The episode I saw took place on a 1960s battleship where the crew starts hearing a clanging coming from the depths of the ocean. They happened to be over the remains of a World War II submarine. One of the sailors aboard the battleship starts feeling then seeing, crew members from the long-sunken submarine urging him to come to them.

The battleship's captain sends a crew member underwater to check out the submarine. The diver does not find any sign of life, but he does find an old, encrusted dog tag that belongs to the sailor who is seeing and hearing things.

The captain talks to the suffering crew member who finally reveals—and relives—how he unwittingly signaled Japanese warships that attacked the submarine and killed all the other crew members. In terrible pain, he wails that it was his fault that the men died and he lived.

The captain grabs the sailor by the shoulders and says something that made me jump to my computer to write this: "It is the time for regret—not guilt."

Every day, I hear people on my radio program expressing "guilt" when it isn't called for.

I hear from parents who feel guilty because one of their offspring is abusing drugs or wasting intellectual and creative potential.

Pointing out that they have other children doing just fine does not allow them to let go of their guilt. And try as I do, it is a struggle to get them to embrace a more appropriate emotion, such as regret, sadness, or even hope that their child will someday find the right path.

Yes, there are situations where guilt is suitable. Such as when parents have abused their children or allowed abuse to occur, when they have been absent and uninvolved, or when they put their own lives before the needs of their children.

All parents occasionally do something for which "regret" is appropriate. However, there are influences and experiences our children have that have nothing to do with us or what we've taught them. No parent can take all the credit for the totality of a child's self-destructiveness or great success.

So the next time you feel guilt, ask yourself, "Am I really the cause of this problem?" Regret, sadness, or disappointment might be more appropriate, but you may have to give up your efforts to make things different.

DR. LAURA SAYS:

"Giving up" can make you feel hopeless, but when it is the right thing to do, you must do it.

Grieving Does Not Always Include Tears

Over the years I have had many people call me out of concern that they are not crying over the death of someone close to them. They wonder if there is something wrong with them psychologically or if something is missing in their character.

This is particularly alarming to married couples when partners grieve in different ways. Men tend to be more stoic, and instead of expressing their emotions, try to fix situations. Women often interpret this as meaning that the men are not "feeling" and just "getting on" when, in reality, the getting-on actions are precisely the way men cope with their equally profound feelings.

Women want their emotional state to be attended to by their men simultaneously with their men expressing their emotions. This is quite a conundrum for men who can't figure out if they are supposed to fall apart or be strong and support their wives.

There's another reason people don't cry when someone dies: Sometimes the deceased simply was not that important to them.

It may be that a parent or sibling was troublesome or never bonded with them in a meaningful way. In fact, they might actually be relieved that that person has passed.

It is also true that in situations where the death was expected for a protracted amount of time, the final, actual loss is not as horrendous as an unexpected death would have been.

In those situations, people have been grieving all along and may be emotionally exhausted by the time death comes. And in those cases we often see people calm at first. Later, the dam breaks and emotions flow. It sometimes takes recovery from the caretaking experience to get busy with the final business of mourning.

Remember: Crying is not an indicator of whether or not a person cares.

If you find yourself withdrawing from normal activities, if you have isolated yourself, or if you are not taking care of yourself, these are indicators that the grief process is not going smoothly. Resorting to drugs or alcohol also points at an attempt to run from feelings.

If you want to cry, feel like you have tears to shed, and just can't, that also suggests that you are having an internal struggle with all the emotions about the lost person. These are the times that joining a grief group or going to a grief counselor might be helpful.

The grieving process varies for each person, and it requires time.

If there is conflict in your marriage in the midst of grieving, talking about your pain and listening carefully to your partner is essential. No judgment, no competing for top sufferer, no blaming, no shutting off from one another.

DR. LAURA SAYS:

Truth and compassion are vital. We need to reach out to each other in times of pain.

Addiction Can Be Beat

One of the most typical, and sad, calls to get on my radio program is the painful plea of a parent, sibling, or spouse for the magic that will make a loved one commit to being clean and sober. Ask any addict, and you will be told there is no such magic. No begging, threatening, preaching, lecturing, crying, yelling, or giving infinite assistance will do the job. It totally comes from within the addict. And the process to get and stay sober is very difficult.

I have gotten a lot of mail over the decades—and I have been on the air often dealing with this subject. Mail complaining that I am too hard on addicts and alcoholics, that I know nothing about addiction.

Some folks have pledged to stop listening to me out of resentment and pure anger—all of which is obviously based on defensiveness.

One such addict wrote:

I even stopped listening to your program for a while because I resented some of the things you would say. But I did return to your program because I really enjoy listening to you.

I was actively listening to your program when I relapsed. During my relapse I began to see what you meant about people with addiction. I was very wrong about you; we addicts and alcoholics can't be completely trusted because it is unlikely we stay sober.

The letter went on:

Relapse is a big issue for people with addiction. It is more likely we will relapse than stay sober, which is unfortunate for our families. Your program has helped me see through the eyes of families with mothers, fathers, daughters, and sons actively using alcohol and drugs. The impact and destruction we addicts cause our families is undeniably harmful to everyone around us.

Loving family members get stuck trying to fix the addict, but in reality unless he or she wants the help it will never happen. Sometimes even if the addict wants it, it is very hard to achieve sobriety. Listening to your program has helped me fight for sobriety because I do not want my daughter or son calling your program because I am destroying their lives. It has helped me see through the eyes of the suffering family.

It then becomes important for addicts to immerse themselves in recovery programs like AA. The commitment often must begin multiple times a day! Addicts need a motivation: no longer wanting to harm their families and/or no longer wanting to harm themselves, for addiction is a self-destructive activity.

One of my personal and dearest friends tells stories about stealing his mother's VCR while she was in the kitchen making him something to eat. He jumped out a window and sold the VCR for drugs. She never let him back in her home—finally.

Today he is 20 years clean and sober, and an amazingly competent, loving, productive, all-around lovable human being.

It can be done.

DR. LAURA SAYS:

The emotions, feelings, memories, and thoughts that the addict is attempting to cover up have to come to the surface and be confronted, embraced, and dealt with in a constructive manner.

Balancing Life in the Face of Death

Sometimes a call to my radio show acts like a complete reboot on life.

One particular caller was in her late forties. She told me, "I have terminal cancer and am conflicted and confused about whether or not I should retire."

This was my first call of the day. She has a job working with the elderly. She has a husband and children. The work, together with the cancer treatment, is making her so terribly tired that when she gets home to family, she has nothing left.

In her exhaustion she said: "I am a lousy wife and lousy mother. I am grumpy and impatient. I don't know what to do."

Ask me how it feels to start my program talking to a woman who was rapidly dying and was trying to figure out how to do it better. As I started the call, I felt focused on helping. During the call, I felt I was touching things way deep inside us all.

I started by pointing out that working herself into exhaustion with the treatment was counterproductive to any quality of life. What is the point of the treatment if we are torturing ourselves in the process of trying to feel normal when nothing will ever be normal again?

"You are pushing yourself into a grave," I said, and she agreed.

It seemed to me that quitting was not the right solution. Her work gave her an important sense of purpose to her life. Without that purpose, life would seem less attractive to continue.

I told her that if she were 85 and tired a lot, she'd have to temper how much work she did. It is a natural part of life that we at some point have to pace ourselves and challenge ourselves differently than when we are younger.

I suggested that she not quit (I could hear her sigh in relief), but she should temper the amount of time at her work. She needed that time and energy for surviving and for family.

I said: "Perhaps two hours a day or two days a week? That way you would continue your work and not feel like your life as you've always known it is over. That is quite depressing, especially facing what you are dealing with."

Frankly, all research demonstrates that when people lose a sense of purpose in life, they lose the motivation to live at all.

Now I got to the second and also very important aspect of her life: family.

"Your work is your purpose; the love from a husband and for children is the basic joy of life," I told her. "You must temper your work and have energy to survive as long as you can and enjoy your life as no longer a grumpy, impatient, lousy wife and mom."

She agreed to all the above and the call ended. I will never forget it.

At the end of the call, I felt good that she believed I had helped her.

And then I cried.

DR. LAURA SAYS:

Whatever time we have, we need to be purposeful and have enjoyment. We need to continue enjoying the love of family and friends.

Moving on After the Painful End of a Friendship

Among the saddest type of caller questions I get on my radio program are those from people dealing with the painful end of a friendship.

The conversation typically starts like this: "We've been friends for 20 years. We've been there for each other through hard times. Nothing in particular happened to end our friendship, but he (or she) has moved on. This is a huge loss for me. Isn't it a huge loss for him (her)?"

When something big and ugly happens to end a friendship, everybody is clear about why there is a rift. It is the quiet, sneaky progression of distance and apathy that takes us by surprise.

Perhaps the friend has started to drink more or indulge in pain medication. Perhaps the friend is having an affair. Perhaps the friend has buddied up with someone who elevates the friend's social status. Perhaps the friend seems to just focus on negatives and spend most of together time in self-indulgent whining. There are many "perhaps" scenarios in the end of a friendship.

You may have tried to be understanding. But you start to realize that this isn't the same person you know as your friend. You try to excuse your friend's behavior. You try and try and try.

The more you try to reconstruct what was, the more you find yourself sinking deeper into an abyss of confusion: "Why doesn't he (she) care as much as I do?"

After that, you start feeling bad about yourself and ask, "Why aren't I worth it to him (her)? How am I so disposable?"

Unfortunately, there is never a satisfying answer. We really don't know why or what is going on in somebody else's head unless the person is willing to be honest and open. We can't fix something when we can't get our hands on the broken parts.

There is a season for all things, including friendship. People change, not always for the better. People make life choices, not always wise ones.

So what do you do? Suffer—for a while.

The loss of an intimate friend with whom you can share everything, who accepts, understands, supports, and nurtures, is devastating. Mourning the loss takes time.

DR. LAURA SAYS:

Keep in mind, though, that one thing hasn't changed: the history you had. Even after the relationship is over, to paraphrase Rick in the classic film *Casablanca*, in a sense, you still "always have Paris."

How Best to Honor Those You've Lost

In the past few years, I've been receiving more calls than usual from people suffering from a loss of someone special: a child, parent, spouse, or dear friend.

That in itself is not surprising, as we are mortal.

What has been different is the degree to which so many people feel and believe that their suffering must include making their life devoid of pleasure, happiness, or success.

I imagine that earlier in our American history, people lived in smaller communities—even big cities had their small, coherent populations—where the cycle of life and death was a part of the fabric of the community.

Townspeople would grieve as a whole and then get on with the business of living, supporting each other through the difficult transition of letting go. There were rules about wearing black and how much time should be spent in mourning, but even those expectations had bona fide end points, after which people were expected to get back into the community life.

Without those "rules and expectations" and without "small, we-all-know-each-other communities," many people are left confused, guilt-ridden, and in pain because of the natural ambivalence about getting on with one's life when someone else is no longer there.

I received a wonderful letter from a woman expressing so eloquently what she learned many years ago from her brother who died of cancer at 22, after 14 surgeries, an amputation, and pharmaceutical attempts to keep him alive since the age of 16.

It seems that he was able to find the loveliness in life despite his death sentence and continual loss of abilities. For example, when he could no longer walk with crutches, he took up lake fishing with his buddies.

When he could no longer fish, he took up being driven by relatives and friends to some of the loveliest vistas America has to offer. Remarkably, he stayed positive—not about his prognosis because he had long accepted the inevitability of his death—but about life as a gift and people as blessings.

Her letter to me was entitled "The Gift," which referred to what she believes she got from her brother in being childlike in wonder every moment of every day to truly appreciate the opportunities of life.

A listener responded to my reading of that letter:

I just heard you read that letter from the gal who lost her 22-year-old brother and how he left her a final gift that she only came to understand after many years of reflection.

You ended with a comment about how we cannot honor the dead by not living our lives; that which they lost we must cherish, respect, embrace, and positively exploit with every fiber of our being.

When I lost my own father, I was lost in my deep grieving and sorrow, at times unable to grasp I will never see him again. One side of my brain told me to live my life to the fullest as my dad did, and enjoy every second. Another part was struggling with that.

I still miss him from the deepest core of my heart and soul. It is so hard.

After hearing you read that letter (and your subsequent comments), I know I must try harder to live my life in the moment and to the fullest. It truly touched me and has made me realize that I must give myself time to grieve and to live my life. I have so much to be thankful for every day and I will be reminding myself of this more.

"Getting on with living" in no way suggests your lack of caring or love for the deceased, or for others also grieving the loss.

Getting on with living is the way you honor the memory and purpose of those who meant something so special to you. Wasting that which they've lost is surely not leaving the world better off for their loss.

DR. LAURA SAYS:

Doing wonderful things with life's options is the way you honor those you miss.

REFLECTIONS

Over the years I have been moved often to tears listening to callers facing life and death situations with courage and even a sense of humor. I can't tell you how many times I wondered if I could ever live up to their attitude and tenacity. Suffering really does bring out the best and worst in each of us.

It is so important to be caring of those who are suffering. They need us, and we need to learn from them. One recent female caller had eight kids and tickets to some new *Avenger* movie. Problem? Her dear friend probably has only four months left to live and asked my caller to go to a hospice-like retreat with her. The caller thought that maybe she should go to the movie with the family, as (1) it was family first, and (2) she made that plan first.

I was shocked and replied that this was the perfect time to teach her kids about sacrifice and compassion. It is understandable that she might not be comfortable with a focus on this . . . but goodness me . . .

Part Four

VALUES

Enjoying the process is success, and winning usually follows.

A mother and her 10-year-old daughter called recently. The little girl explained that on the last day of school everyone brings a T-shirt in and all the friends and teachers write on it. She didn't wish to mess up her own T-shirt, so she took one from her sister without asking and lied to her mother and sister about it. She called because her mother made her give $20 to her sister for a new T-shirt and said she could not go to a birthday party the upcoming weekend. She wanted to know if this punishment was fair.

She was incredibly articulate, and I told her I would talk to her like she was an adult. "The T-shirt is really not the issue. The fact is that you didn't care if you upset your sister when you already knew she didn't want you to take her clothes without permission . . . and you didn't care that your parents would see you as a lying thief. The issue is you not caring about anyone's feelings in your family."

Silence.

So I asked her how it would feel to her if no one in her family cared at all about her feelings.

"That would be terrible. I would not like it," was her response. Silence again. She got it.

I told her that her mother forgot one more consequence (mom still on line) . . . T-shirt is to be destroyed. The little girl actually thanked me. There is hope.

CHAPTER TWELVE

Your Values Reality Check

Honor and integrity determine your worth—not things or popularity.

You Made an Awful Choice.
Now Move Past the Guilt.

According to a Reuter's health report, half of the American women who would rather not get pregnant will have an unplanned pregnancy each year. This is not because they are poor and uneducated and don't know about condoms. They simply don't bother to use any form of contraceptive.

The National Center for Health Statistics recently reported there are almost 6.4 million pregnancies per year in the United States. Forty-five percent were to women who were not married. And there were 1.22 million abortions.

Casual "wasting" of human beings is a horrible state of affairs for a population imagining itself civilized.

I took a recent call from "Jennifer" that demonstrated this mentality, and the inevitable terrible consequences. She told me that she's had an issue for the past two years.

"This sounds horrible; I'm just . . . I'm embarrassed still. I had an abortion two years ago. My boyfriend at the time is now my husband."

I asked her why she had an abortion after a year and a half of dating. She replied that she already had a three-year-old daughter from a prior "relationship" and aborted "just because."

"You didn't know about birth control? You'd already had an unintended pregnancy, so why were you having sex with no birth control?"

"I was being stupid. I didn't really care at the time."

This is the situation with many young women these days since abortion became birth control and feminism took away the special nature of a woman and her intimacy with a man willing to commit to her and be obligated to their lives together.

The problem is that real women feel terrible pain after killing their in-utero children. And that was the point of Jennifer's call. After being irresponsible about contraception, sexual intimacy, and abortion, she now was married and the mother of two little girls and was suffering over her decision to abort.

"I don't know what to do. I obsess over it still . . . every day. I go online. I look at pictures [of aborted babies] just to make myself feel worse. I don't know why I do this. But it's like I'm obsessed with this whole thing, and I can't let it go."

"Okay, Jennifer, let me put it to you bluntly."

"Okay."

"You did a horribly irresponsible and disgusting thing."

"Yeah."

"And you should feel guilt forever for what you've done. You were frivolous with a human life to suit yourself. You didn't want to stop and use a condom because you didn't want to lose your boyfriend. So what you did was horrendous. You cannot change it. Forcing yourself to suffer over it doesn't ever change it—the baby is still dead."

I'm sure every reader is now aghast at what seems like cruelty—and I understand your reaction. I had it too as I heard myself talk! However, you must see that what I depicted was the truth—and the first part of repentance is dealing with the truth and taking responsibility for it. Step two is where the compassion comes in.

"Jennifer, you have two children and you owe them. And there's something you can do about them—while there is nothing you can do about the abortion. So, spending any time punishing yourself takes away from how good a mother you can be to them. It's selfish of you to obsess about suffering. Use that energy to be a very good mother."

She asked, "So, just try to forget about it completely? Like it never happened?"

I answered, "You can't and shouldn't forget about it. But you have a family to take care of. To spend your time punishing yourself in the hopes you can get over the guilt is self-serving. Now you have to serve your family—not your guilt, your family. Take all the guilt energy and put it into doing your best to raise these girls to do better. That's the only way I can see you making up for this."

Happily, she said, "All right. Thank you so much, Dr. Laura."

DR. LAURA SAYS:

Too many people in reasonable positions of leadership (parents, teachers, clergy) avoid calling for appropriate guilt for inappropriate behaviors. However, in our politically correct environment, nothing is deemed wrong! With that philosophy we can never exonerate true, righteous guilt and help guide folks to a better path.

The Not-So-Fine Taste of Whine

I just don't know what I'd do if I didn't have license to whine about outrageous fortunes, betrayals, hurts, slights, annoyances, or just a bad-hair day. I generally prescribe somewhere between a day and a half to five days of pure outright whining, whimpering, and downright self-indulgent "poor me" time. I consider it a kind of cathartic experience.

Whining allows for some venting of reasonable and righteous pain, disappointment, fear, frustration, or frank rage. I'm all for whining as a relatively benign form for the expression of furiously negative emotions—it's much better than battery or booze.

It is staying stuck in whining mode that can become a short-term or lifelong serious problem. It's healthy to vent occasionally, but endless rumination on the negative keeps you paralyzed in misery, reinforces hopelessness, and demoralizes those around you, who feel completely helpless to bring any happiness back into your life.

Sometimes, continuous whining is seen as the only means of "getting back" at people or situations that have hurt you. Other times, whining is seen as all that's left to do in a life of sorrow.

Ultimately, though, whining has no power to water the flowers and bring back the pleasurable sights and sounds of a life worth living. That's why I wrote the book *Stop Whining, Start Living.* No matter what you've suffered or continue to suffer, while you are alive, you have the opportunity to get something from this life.

It is often quite difficult to make the decision to give up whining and suffering, because that sort of behavior gives you a breather from having to persevere and gets you a bit of sympathy.

I prefer to encourage whiners to reject negative thoughts, emotions, and attitudes. Then they can shift perspective, open up to gratitude and goodness, and embrace obligations to loved ones and the world in general. Before long, just doing what you're supposed to be doing—instead of moaning about why you can't or won't or shouldn't fulfill your responsibilities—will have you feeling better about yourself and will uplift your interactions with others in incredible ways.

A famous rabbi once said, "Despair is a cheap excuse for avoiding one's purpose in life. And a purpose in life is the best way to avoid despair."

Transitioning from pain to perspective in thought and emotion does not happen automatically. Believe me, sometimes you really have to make a Herculean effort to force yourself into it. It is much easier to stay with the enraged defense against whatever assault has occurred than raise your gaze toward the sky and feel gratitude for being alive. Being alive gives you alternatives and the opportunity for solace and renewed joy.

As an example, a recent female caller to my radio show complained that her husband "almost" had an affair. She was ferocious in her anger, whining with self-pity and generally not in the mood to look at this situation any other way than as a victim. I pointed out that it was "almost," that he chose to be with her and the family, and that he was honest about his motivation. I practically had to use a battering ram to get into her head the point that he loves her but he was hungry for her love and warmth—both of which she admitted she'd not been giving him. Her whining was to hide her guilt, her culpability in starving him to the point where he was sifting through trash.

She had two choices: high horse (whining) or loving marriage (perspective).

I hope she chose wisely.

DR. LAURA SAYS:

Perspective is everything.

Live with Reality (Enjoy the Meatballs)

Sometimes you have to know when to hush up, shut up, or just let certain things go.

I am a big supporter of standing up for values and standing up for friends. I disdain people's cowardice in being more concerned with how they look or who is going to be mad at them when a moment obviously calls for standing up and being heard.

Yet I find myself telling callers more frequently to "stifle" themselves, in the immortal terms of Archie Bunker. Why? How can this be?

Let me give you some examples.

Unfortunately, grandmother favoritism is a frequent complaint of my callers. They often describe in gruesome detail how many more gifts and how much more attention their mother-in-law gives to her other grandchildren than to theirs—or to the non-adopted child or non-stepchild.

Callers want to know what to say to change the behavior and stop hurting the children. They want magic from me, and there just isn't any.

I explain that some people are simply small-minded or small-hearted; that some people are bigoted and self-centered; that some people just don't care that they cause pain—even to a child. Some people are just that way. No conversation is going to change anything.

Fighting constantly with that person, or with your spouse over that person, is useless. I recommend simply avoiding people who hurt children, regardless of their problem. Children should not be exposed to the destructive influences of cruel favoritism.

"That means that the child she is nice to loses out?" they ask.

"No," I tell them, "the child who she (he) is not cruel to doesn't lose out on anything. That child gains a sense of the importance of family loyalty, fairness, and not 'selling out oneself' for personal gain. Learning of this sort needs to start early."

Then there are the relatives who always seem to be annoyances at family gatherings. I always suggest never confronting them. These people have superior war tactics, and since other relatives have shown their unwillingness to deal with such difficult individuals, you must "stifle yourself."

Two people cannot argue unless both participate. If someone baits you and you smile, make a nice, complimentary statement, and excuse yourself to chat with other people at the gathering, there can be no fight.

You think this is going to make you feel like "they won—you lost"? Think again. You've kept your dignity, lowered your blood pressure, acted sanely, and kept the ugliness from overcoming you. They didn't win a thing. Everybody knows what they're about. And since no one is going to deal with it, you shouldn't either.

Other callers want to have confrontations with people who have not changed and are not likely to change. They yearn for something closer when nothing closer is likely to be possible. They then rattle back and forth from confrontation and begging to excommunication.

I tell these folks to face reality: There are only two meatballs in your spaghetti, even though you desperately want six. You can argue about it, but the number of meatballs won't change; so you can eat nothing, or you can enjoy the reality of what is.

That means that when dealing with family or friends who are quite limited in what they can or are willing to offer, you have that same spaghetti-and-meatball choice. Change your desperate expectations, enjoy the meatballs that are there, and you ultimately will be a happier person.

DR. LAURA SAYS:

I believe in a good fight when it protects the innocent. Trying to make people be other than who they are is not a worthy direction for your energies.

Look at Yourself Before Blaming Others

During my daily radio call-in program, I receive many sensitive calls. One male caller, for instance, called to tell me he's been separated for two years and has a girlfriend who is divorced with four kids. Evidently, the oldest teenage daughter of his girlfriend has accused him of touching her inappropriately. According to him, this was not true.

Assuming he is being honest with me, this girl knows what to say to abort this relationship in order to refocus mom on the kids. Research indicates that children of a divorced mom are better off when mom does not remarry, shack up, or get otherwise invested in some new love. They've already lost one parent to visiting status; they don't need their custodial parent to get distracted by lust and romance. Besides, second marriages have a higher failure rate than first marriages!

I asked him why, with two minor children, he is separated. He said, "Because it wasn't good. It wasn't always bad, though."

I came back at him with, "Divorce is always bad for the kids; they have their lives pulled in two opposing directions and end up competing for attention with new spouses and new half-siblings or stepsiblings. I think you might have considered increasing the 'good' and tolerating the 'bad' for the sake of the kids." He virtually shrugged that off.

I suggested that he immediately stop seeing this woman (he might end up in jail and then as a registered sex offender), not date while he is still married (take this opportunity to examine himself and change what would benefit the marriage and family), and use his time to take care of and raise his own children.

You could almost see his bottom lip jutting out in a pout.

In my opinion, too many people push aside their responsibilities for the opportunity to just feel good in general or about themselves through the melodrama of a new heart-fluttering romance.

Another male caller was divorced after 22 years of marriage, with the last 10 rocky and the last 5 as roommates. He called because he has "problems with his current girlfriend."

He found someone who is a closet alcoholic, no friends, no family relationships, and is belligerent when pushed. "I met her after she broke up with her ex, who just liked to push her buttons," he said. "I am helping her."

He was totally consumed by her problems—and frankly, grateful for them. Why? When people don't want to face their own problems, they often find someone with blatant problems to focus on. He becomes a hero, savior, and martyr—all of which make him automatically feel better about himself after his previous marital failure. Now he doesn't have to examine his own contribution to his failed marriage. By contrast with this current girlfriend, he appears the healthy, okay one. Additionally, a woman this messed up will not challenge him in any real ways that would undermine his fantasy that his ex-wife was the problem.

So let's look at the issues.

- Emotions have no IQ—most decisions are better made from your good sense.

- To tap into that good sense, stand back and wonder aloud if you'd advise someone dear to you to follow your path or not. If your answer to yourself is NO, then don't do it yourself in spite of any "But . . ." you can come up with.
- Examine your motivations. Are you focusing in on so-called rights or desires and pushing down your responsibilities and obligations to others?

DR. LAURA SAYS:

In the long run, you will be happier with yourself and life if you're proud of yourself—which you won't be if you don't sacrifice and try to contribute more than you take for yourself.

REFLECTIONS

Interestingly enough, only good people feel guilt. Most people seem to have a misconception about what guilt is. I explain that guilt is a feeling or awareness that they have done something immoral, unethical, or illegal. Otherwise, it probably isn't guilt. It could simply be SADNESS. For example: I feel guilty that my sister makes less money than I do and demands money from me and our mother and I don't want to give her anymore. That isn't guilt, although my sister may be trying to convince me that I'm not a good sister because I won't give her what she wants. It isn't guilt. It is frustration, anger, or sadness. Guilt blames the self, while those other reactions require you to confront reality. Some people are so afraid and uncomfortable talking about REAL things, problems, and feelings, that they would be more likely to blame themselves.

CHAPTER THIRTEEN

Personal Responsibility

You know what I LOVE about responsibility? It gives you the power to be the architect of your own life. Now if you don't use or abuse the concept of responsibility . . . please don't blame or complain: Learn.

Have Some Shame, Please

In a recent newspaper letter to the editor, a well-known television personality told the story of her teen pregnancy. She'd gotten pregnant out of wedlock at 17, and wrote that she had to endure her mother's disappointment, her father's anger, and the priest's admonition.

The shame and ridicule were more than she could bear. She wrote, "I was no good. I had messed up. I knew it. My dreams and life were shattered. Days later, I was married off and sent away. I said I did not love this man. I was told, 'You made your bed; now you must lie in it.'"

She went on to recount the damage to her self-esteem, which she called "life threatening," and described being ostracized and condemned as a bad girl, though she had tried all her life to do well and make her parents proud.

Naturally, I feel compassion for her. She suffered because of the negative reactions of the significant adults in her life. But this situation was not all about her. It also was about the innocent, dependent baby that found itself in a tenuous situation: a chaotic environment where its parents were unprepared, uncommitted, immature teenagers having a sexual relationship, but they were unprepared for the biological consequences.

And it seems as if this person still doesn't get it.

Feeling shame for behaviors that a community considers generally unacceptable is a most uncomfortable experience, but its purpose is to dissuade people from situations that cause pain to themselves and to others.

The motivation behind those, like the letter writer, who rail against shame is clearly to disassociate behaviors from consequences.

They feel that judgment is a bad thing because it hurts feelings. But hurt feelings as a result of actions that hurt others are a good thing. They're part of having a conscience. Only good people feel guilt. Only good people suffer from doing ill to others.

Suffering over doing wrong is human, natural, expected, and respected. To complain that wrongdoing to others should not result in any negative reaction is ultimately immature, defensive, and contrary to the notion of taking responsibility for how one's actions impact others.

The TV personality complained about having to marry a young man she didn't love in order to legitimize the baby and take responsibility as a family for the child's welfare. Why is that a bad thing? Why was she having sexual relations with someone she didn't have the highest regard for and wouldn't choose to be the father of her inevitable children? Is it not in the best interest of the child to have the foundation of a family? And of course, there was the adoption option.

Submitting to responsibility for a dependent child seems like a noble action to me. Staying mutually committed for the well-being of another human being sounds noble to me!

Of course, people with noble intentions generally don't undertake marriages this young. Adoption is often the best solution for children of these relationships—but I digress.

The author of this letter was making the points that the media should not focus on those young men and women who make this sort of "mistake," because it hurts their feelings and because these are private issues.

Generally, these are private issues. However, when people in the public eye and arena, and their families, display behaviors that undermine role-modeling obligations or expectations, it should be examined publicly because impressionable youngsters take their cues from their environment. When there is no public shame for destructive, hurtful, or illegal behaviors, our children see and emulate them, and the disasters grow exponentially.

So instead of lamenting how upsetting it is to be embarrassed being a pregnant youngster, it is important to point out to all the other youngsters out there what dangerous ground they tread when they walk as responsible adults, yet leave the footprints of naïve children.

Taking this story public is a fantastic way to warn children away from playing with the perks of a committed adult when they are in no position to take on responsibilities for their actions or cope well with the emotional fallout.

DR. LAURA SAYS:

We are in an era that judges judgment itself as evil. It isn't. Morals, values, principles, and ethics protect against pain and destruction.

"Doing" Is So Much More Important Than Simply "Trying"

One of the most annoying responses I get on my SiriusXM 111 radio program to a suggestion to help with a problem is, "I will try." What do you mean you are going to try? According to Yoda from *Star Wars*, there is no trying, only doing.

What do people really mean when they agree to try? Is it a commitment to not working hard, taking risks, suffering discomfort, or following through? Trying means that you are going to give it some level of attention or effort in action, but at the first sign of blowback or discomfort, you are going to quit but be able to put your conscience at ease by uttering, "At least I tried."

The difference between trying and actually doing is that when doing, one stays with it regardless of the consequences or the reactions of others.

That's the most important aspect of doing versus trying. The second aspect is that in trying, your whole focus is on having someone else change. A wife or a husband might try to keep things pleasant and light for an evening and then watch critically for the spouse to change. When the wife or husband doesn't experience that instant gratification, the trying is over. The idea was a failure.

Doing is to change yourself whether or not the other person parallels your actions. It is important, for example, for a man to behave like a gentleman even if the woman in question is a pain in the butt. One must never let the actions of others dictate the quality of our character, choices, or behaviors.

Doing the right thing without experiencing success or gratitude is the mark of a strong person with weighty character.

Recently a couple called, with the wife telling me that her husband goes in and out of saying he's not happy and wants a divorce; they have two children 9 and 15. He has a child from a prior marriage who is now 19. When he spoke, he sounded like a petulant teenager, saying, "I don't feel appreciated all the time."

I told him that nobody on earth feels or receives appreciation all the time and that every time he had a "feeling," it perhaps should be accepted as transient and not used to abuse his wife with threats of divorce that also upset and frighten the children.

I reminded him he already wrecked the world of his 19-year-old with that divorce. Hurting two more children was not acceptable. Meanwhile, his wife told me that she spends a lot of time trying to fix his mood.

I explained clearly to him that he was being cruel and frightening the children all in the name of a feeling. "A man has a moral obligation to behave properly in spite of feelings that come and go. It is simply something he must do."

Doing is a commitment; trying is not. Doing represents effort toward a goal and a willingness to suffer along the way if need be; trying does not promise any of that.

What happens next is your weakness takes over. The intelligence behind the healthy choice is shrouded with the inability to move on, so you "try" again—knowing you will come to this desperate place yet again and again.

DR. LAURA SAYS:

Trying is too often a game one plays with one's own mind and life. When you really know something has to be dealt with but you don't want the loss, sadness, or confrontation, then you "give it a try."

Valuing Right and Wrong
Is the Right Thing to Do

I had two remarkable calls to my radio program recently. The first was remarkable not for its uplifting value, but for its cheekiness, naïveté, and dangerous loss of perspective.

A 20-year-old woman called to ask a question about her fiancé. I always "interrogate" callers before they ask me their questions because often the questions are not the callers' actual issues. In this case, I discovered that the woman's fiancé was 22, they'd been dating for two years, and they were shacking up at her divorced mother's home.

I asked, "If you want to live together as man and wife with all the perks that come from that, why didn't you just go to a justice of the peace and get married?"

"Because I want a nice wedding," she sweetly replied.

"You mean a traditional white-dress wedding?" I asked. She said yes.

I said, "So you want a traditional wedding, which celebrates the commitment between two people who are going to become one in body and soul, but you're shacking up and having out-of-wedlock sex while living with a guy who can't even afford a little apartment, so you're living under your mother's roof without paying rent . . . this is your idea of 'traditional'?"

There was stunned and annoyed silence at the other end of the phone, so I asked, "Do you plan to also have your sons and daughters shack up in your home rather than marry?"

She said she did not. I inquired as to why, and there was another annoyed silence.

She made noises as if she might hang up, but I pressed on. "What is your problem with your fiancé?"

"He financially supports his mother and all his siblings. They live in a nice home. I don't think he should be doing that because we will need that money to have a home of our own," she said.

"My dear," I told her, "he is going to continue supporting his family because that is his primary commitment. So I suggest you make a deal with your mother to pay rent and continue living in her home with your future husband, or find a small apartment that doesn't cost much, because you're going to have to budget to support his mom and siblings first. That's the kind of wonderful guy you have!"

At least she was polite when she hung up.

The second call was from a 24-year-old who wanted to complain about her relationship with her mother and how she doesn't want the same for her relationship with her three small children.

She told me that her mother was negative and would hurt her feelings being critical, saying things like, "Your situation is due to your own stupidity."

It turns out that the three children had two different fathers, and the caller had never married either one of the men.

I asked what about her mother's comment wasn't spot-on? There was stunned silence.

"My dear," I said, "your children are in chaos with your multiple relationships and out-of-wedlock births. I think the beginning of you not having an estranged relationship with your children, as you have with your mother, is to own up to your mistakes. Instead of labeling her assessment of your behavior and circumstances negative and critical, tell her that she's accurate and that you need her support now to bring stability to your children's lives."

These two young women sadly represent the status of young people today—no firm sense of right and wrong, propriety, modesty, integrity, or forethought. Their parents and our society have

let them down, supporting the notions that values are simply sub-
jective, negative judgments, and that what you feel at the moment
is your best measure for making decisions.

The first young woman is trapped by her pseudo-commitment
of shacking up. She doesn't have the luxury of objectivity and will
probably marry, be angry, have children, and divorce. The second
young lady may very well search for another guy to give her the
fantasy of a happy home, as she has unprotected sex with him to
affirm his attachment and have yet another child.

We might excuse both young women's behaviors due to
underlying emotional "issues," but in the past, value judgments,
shame, and morals have always served to protect young people.

DR. LAURA SAYS:

We need our values back!

When You Make a Mistake, Own It

I participated in a sailboat race with a crew of four others, which
lasted 10 hours and covered 81 miles of open sea. The officials
at the finish line who recorded the time of crossing incorrectly
surmised that we failed to go around a light buoy that was part
of the course.

They then gave us a designation that ultimately meant we
hadn't completed the race at all. Let's just say I was severely
miffed at this blatant incompetence.

Two heavy-hitter sailors on my boat remedied the situation,
after frustration on both sides. (Happily, folks on two other boats
that finished along with us spoke up on our behalf.)

I waited a few days and sent a most gracious letter to the fellow in charge, who originally made the decision to "do the wrong thing"—that is, make an assessment without concrete proof.

In my letter, I made light of the situation, leaving the door seriously wide open for an apology. Instead, his response tried to slap me silly with little pieces of misinformation, to avoid taking any sincere responsibility for the fiasco.

Okay, I'd had it.

In my follow-up letter, I wrote: "You keep reminding me you are the pro—part of being such is having the character to own it when you're wrong. You were wrong and you should simply have apologized. When I mess up, I own it and say, 'I'm sorry.' I don't turn specious accusations against the person to resurrect my appearance."

Short and simple, he wrote back, "If you feel you need an apology, I'm sorry for any distress I may have caused you." If? May? Is he kidding?

This is what causes the disintegration of many a relationship. People often make mistakes or behave inappropriately. But unlike that stupid movie of the 1970s, love should always mean saying that you're sorry. And "sorry" should come without one single qualifying word, phrase, information, or argument.

Many people have a problem with apologizing because they still are stuck in their childhoods, when being wrong made them feel stupid, weak, or vulnerable.

Well, too bad. That's the price of being human: being accountable for your actions and understanding their impact.

Relationships often break down when they don't have to, simply because people refuse to take responsibility for their actions. Instead of simply "owning it," one tries to expose the ill doings of the other, possibly even blaming the other for provoking you into whatever it is that you did that was wrong.

There's an irony here, too: You don't want to look bad to the other person—so you argue the person into the ground to justify or exonerate yourself. And in so doing, you become the "bad one" in the person's mind.

So, struggle against your self-defensiveness, and—in spite of any real or imagined contributing factors—just say, "My bad. I'm sorry. I was angry, but I should not have said/done what I did. I regret hurting you. How might I make it up to you?" When you do this, the other person will hold you in higher esteem, feel justified in his or her pain by your admission (and that reduces rage), and feel that you "give a damn."

Apologizing properly is probably one of the most important aspects of a quality relationship, because "stuff happens," inadvertently or intentionally, and it is essential that repairs are made, or the leaks could sink the relationship forever.

True repentance has several parts: first, responsibility; second, true remorse; third, repair; and fourth, no repeat. The next time you hurt somebody, even accidentally, please just own up to it—admit you did it. You can explain yourself, but never to dismiss the hurt. Try to repair the damage, and think to yourself and express to the person how it won't be repeated.

DR. LAURA SAYS:

Lingering angst, resentment, and dislike can easily be wiped away with a sincere "I am sorry."

Don't Shack Up—Shape Up!

I've had innumerable calls from women who clearly are somewhere between ambivalent and confused—stuck between the value-free feminist education they've gotten from a society adrift from its sensible moorings and their innermost heart's desires for committed love.

One caller to my radio program has three children, each from a different man, including the third with her current "shack-up." Talk about an identity crisis. Imagine what life is like for these three children with three dads and very little security.

The caller was complaining that her current guy had been unfaithful. I immediately told her that shack-ups have no such expectation of fidelity and that he had the freedom to have sexual relationships with whomever he pleased.

"But we have a child together," she insisted.

"Well," I countered, "it is sad for the child that his mother decided a third time to have a child out of wedlock with a man who did not make any pretense of vows of loyalty, fidelity, or love as part of a sacrament."

She was stupefied. She couldn't imagine that all arrangements between men and women don't have the same value, meaning, consequences, or inherent benefits.

"I'll bet," I continued, "that you thought the only difference between shacking up and marriage was a piece of paper. Well, there is a reason men in particular shack up: less obligations and responsibilities and the freedom to do what they wish."

She then wanted to know what she should do. Here's where I have a problem. I have to ask women to sacrifice their happiness for the well-being of their children. I told her to suck it up, smile a lot, use a condom so she won't contract a venereal disease from him, and try to keep the home life peaceful and consistent for the children.

I reminded her that what she's done to these three children's lives and psyches is far more desperate and destructive than his having a dalliance.

In my final comments to her, I said: "A marriage license is not just a piece of paper. All you did was to get a guy willing to cohabit and not have to use a condom for sex without commitment. In a marriage, two people make solemn vows to each other—ones they usually keep."

Her feminist upbringing told her that having babies out of wedlock, having sex whenever interested, and cohabiting to keep freed from obligation were all good things. Unfortunately, they're not. They are in direct opposition to the innermost longing of people to belong to somebody who is making it his or her life's mission to love, cherish, protect, and be faithful.

There is a conflict inside women who are taught one thing by the liberal feminist mentality in our schools and our culture, but who feel something quite different in their inherent drive to bond, nurture, and nest.

There is a reason there is documentation that shack-ups lead to more "infidelity," mental illness, breakups, and violence.

DR. LAURA SAYS:

It simply isn't marriage when folks don't know each other that well, or make uninformed decisions about commitment, or decide to cohabit with the tentativeness of someone trying on shoes, or are constantly taking the temperature of the relationship to see how they like it.

RELECTIONS

Every day on my radio program I urge people to stand up for their values. I warn them that there will be a cost—sometimes even a high cost—but that the quality of any culture is determined by what it stands for and holds dear. Your values should never be compromised simply because they may seem outdated or if they fall out of favor with what's trendy or what others think—even if your friends shun you. We all have to answer to ourselves. Here's the bottom line: The less you stand up for values, the fewer values there will be for anyone to live by.

CHAPTER FOURTEEN

It All Starts with You

My son, at 10, was doing the New Year's Day broadcast with me. His job was to answer caller's questions with me. His answer to one caller flabbergasted us all: YOU ARE THE ARCHITECT OF YOUR OWN LIFE. Wow!

A New Year's Resolution: Explore the Beauty You Bring to Others

New Year's resolutions: Should we make them; how to stick with them? Boring and largely useless.

Here's an entirely new idea. How about making a list of the courageous, generous, kind, thoughtful, touching, and loving things you did and also recognize what other people did.

I am sick and tired of the notion of waking up every January 1 with someone imagining we all have to take an inventory of our shortcomings. Frankly, it's okay to have shortcomings; it is entirely human. I never really got how folks were supposed to be motivated by negativity and reflecting on their failures. It seems more reasonable to me for people to explore what beauty they have brought to others and the world through thoughts and deeds.

This is even more obvious with marriages. If you have ever been to couples or marriage therapy, you know it starts with everyone's complaints—then the hurt, embarrassment, and defensiveness. I never understood how that was going to motivate either spouse to be or do better. It must feel more like a kid dragged into the principal's office for punishment.

How about starting counseling or each discussion with all the good things that can possibly be brought up. Rather than saying "You never spend time with me/kids/washing floors, etc.," as a way of motivating a husband, try:

"Honey, I love watching you with the kids. It reminds me of how utterly wonderful you are."

Or "Honey, I'm a bit backed up. Would you take care of the floor today for me? Besides, I like to watch your back muscles flex while you swing that mop."

Or "Honey, I miss you close to me. Want to take a quiet or maybe not so quiet shower with me later?"

Can you possibly imagine stirring up hurt, embarrassment, or defensiveness with this seductive approach?

And for you men:

"Sweetie, I got you this lipstick because it reminds me of the color you wore when we first met. I just love that memory."

Can you imagine a wife complaining about how strenuous her day was so she has no time to fuss with her makeup? No, I don't think so.

Or "You are the light of my life, and I love you deeply. I miss having quiet, silly, and sexy time with you. I appreciate how much you do for the kids and the house, but I would like to have the time with you as we used to so that you could laugh and have the good times."

I think you get the idea. Sell whatever you want in the form of a gift to the other. Make doing what you'd like to have the spouse do a win for the spouse. Treat any request as a treasure the other cannot deny himself or herself.

Oh, are you thinking this is manipulation? Well, you are right—it is. However, manipulation designed to benefit another is certainly not selfish even though you can rejoice in the shared experience. Loving, thoughtful, kind, and caring manipulations are the stuff of love.

It can be frustrating when you can't control everything and everyone (spouses and kids) so that your perception of going smoothly is realized. It takes a wise and thoughtful spouse, family member, or friend to twist it all about so that you can again feel the joy of life.

DR. LAURA SAYS:

Sometimes with all that piles up in life we all can lose sight of joy and become mired in the routine and responsibilities.

The Right Way to Bring Comfort to Others

Have you noticed that when you try to make upset people feel better, it usually doesn't work? You are almost guaranteed a failure—good intentions not withstanding—if you try to make them look at the bright side, tell them that they should be grateful for what they have, or point out that other people have it worse.

A woman called my radio program profoundly upset that her husband didn't want more children. Her husband felt strongly that two children were enough. She was devastated.

I gently pointed out that she had two healthy children, that the Tenth Commandment points to being grateful for what you have and not covet, and that we can't always have everything we want in life. She begrudgingly acknowledged these truths, but it didn't ease her painful disappointment one bit.

I told her that when I turned 60—that very morning—I woke up, sat straight up in bed, and proclaimed I wanted a baby. I meant it. Anyway, I told the caller that I had that disappointment and sadness every day because I wouldn't be having more children, and it is a letdown, especially when I go out and see cute little kids.

I pointed out to her that it is a burden she'd have to carry forever. It was at that point that she began to softly cry; she realized that her pain was real and acknowledged by someone else.

When you try to make people feel better about their hurts without giving validation to the reasonableness of their pain, they just don't cross that bridge to acceptance. Without that crossing, the "good news" about their blessings just doesn't stick.

Too many times people try to comfort others by telling them basically that they have no reason to feel bad. That just isn't true, and it isn't nice.

It is important to give acknowledgment to the right and reasonableness of being hurt or disappointed. It is this understanding that makes people feel validated in their pain and leads the way to healing.

When you try to bring comfort to someone, please first find a way to acknowledge those bad feelings. Without doing that, people feel like they are not supposed to feel what indeed they are feeling. They simply can't move on without that all-important step.

DR. LAURA SAYS:

Sad feelings count, too.

The Sad Pursuit of Perfection

The perfect body . . . or your life? That's essentially the question raised in a new survey of British undergraduates. Surprisingly, nearly one-third of the young women said they would trade at least a year of their lives to have a perfect body.

The survey found that 16 percent of them would trade a year, and another 10 percent were willing to give 2 to 5 years, while 2 percent would trade up to 10 years of life away. And 1 percent said they would even give up 21 or more years.

It seems as though today's youth consider the perfect appearance more important than qualities such as kindness, honesty, a sense of humor, or intelligence. It's all about the way they look.

In fact, according to the American Society of Plastic Surgeons, more than 326,000 children age 18 and younger had cosmetic procedures in 2004 to correct something that made them self-conscious.

Now I believe that if something is broken, fix it if you can. That's why I support a child's desire (not a parent's pressure) to pin back large ears (otoplasty), to correct breast asymmetry or reduce enlarged male breasts (gynecomastia), and reshape a nose (rhinoplasty), which is the most common procedure among teens since noses reach their final form between ages 13 and 16.

What horrifies me is that some plastic surgeons will perform liposuctions and breast enlargements on kids. They will also inject Botox and other fillers into children. These procedures aim to make children appear more like adults and relate to issues of sexuality—not self-confidence.

Yet even when plastic surgery procedures address quality-of-life issues, children, by virtue of their lack of maturity and propensity toward magical thinking, may have exaggerated notions of how these procedures will improve their lives.

Physicians and parents need to confirm that the child is realistic about what these changes can and will do for them. And we need to be aware that our culture is teaching our children to revere appearance over character. And that is clearly not a good thing.

I laughed heartily upon reading a report on the toy doll Barbie. This doll has been the center of controversy, with critics insisting that young girls will develop unrealistic ideas of body image based on the doll's appearance. That's not the funny part.

I laughed because Barbie's waistline is proportionally 39 percent smaller than the average anorexic patient's, and her fat-to-body mass ratio is below the 17 percent required to menstruate.

Researchers generated a computer model of an adult woman with Barbie doll proportions, discovering that her back could not support her body, and her body would be too narrow to contain more than half a liver and just a few centimeters of intestine. Such a woman would die of malnutrition.

Now that I think of it, that really isn't funny at all.

DR. LAURA SAYS:

Teach your children that beauty is lovely . . . goodness is beautiful.

Time to Reinvent Yourself

In the iconic movie *The Way We Were* with Robert Redford and Barbra Streisand, the question was asked, "Can't we go back to how it was—how we were?" The answer, obviously, was no.

It's true in relationships, health, careers, hobbies—in fact, in every human endeavor. Why? Because life is not complacently static; time allows for the intricate complexities of life. A recent caller to my radio show described being frustrated and depressed for years. She did not identify herself but did explain she was very big in the music industry. Her success had waned, and she spent every day trying to go back to "the way it was." "I am killing myself every day, struggling to re-create what I had. I am miserable, and it seems so hopeless," she explained.

The caller had seen a recent post to my Facebook page showing a lovely photo of a woman with the ocean in the background. In her hand were scores of tiny seashells that were gently falling onto the sand at her feet. The caption read, "Sometimes you have to accept the fact that certain things will never go back to how they used to be." It was right on point.

She was taken by that coincidence and more sadly offered that she was driving herself crazy trying to restore her career and life. I suggested that she drop the word "restore" and replace it with "reinvent." She repeated the two words side by side a number of times and then went silent as though truly, deeply considering what that would mean. I worried that she might perceive this shift as giving up, a resignation. Happily, she did not. She started up again saying, "Well, that is an interesting way to look at it."

She's right. After all, you have certain talents. In the past you used them one particular way, but now you have the opportunity to use them in other ways. Reinvent yourself, as none of us can ever restore the past.

If you were a skier and tore up your knee permanently, there would be no going back to Olympic trials. If you were a wife whose beloved husband passed, you could never experience his loving glances across the dinner table. Once you age and can no longer hang in physically with younger sports competitors, you have to accept your limitations. All of this is simply life.

I suggested she explore some other way to express and enjoy her talents—teaching, performing on the Internet, writing music for others.

She actually became noticeably energized right then and there. She had an attainable goal. And with that recognition came enthusiasm and hope. Challenges are an opportunity to enrich your life. People often are afraid to let go of what is so familiar to them, even if it hurts—like this caller's years of trying to "restore" her past. Their argument is that at least they have something; if they let go, they will have nothing. And that is true—but only temporarily. Yes, there will be a void. And that is the point! You must let go to allow for that void because the void is a space created for opportunity.

If you don't let go of a bad relationship, you don't afford yourself the opportunity to be in a good relationship. It takes courage and such insight to realize that there is no change without some fear, some doubt, and a lot of discomfort. But the upside is that opportunity appropriately approached can remedy the quality of your life.

DR. LAURA SAYS:

Take this moment to think about how you keep trying to no avail to push the sand back up the hill. Think then of a better way to use your energies and abilities. Reinvent yourself.

Yes We Can . . . Choose Our Mood

Depressed?

While it is a fact that some people struggle with the psychiatric disorder of clinical depression, it is also true that many others actually have a choice in their moods.

That may surprise, or even anger, many of you. You may imagine that you have absolutely no control over how you feel, and don't want to be blamed for your state of mind.

For those of you so struck, consider this a good-news, bad-news message. The good news is that you actually have the power to shift your thoughts and mood from negative to positive.

The bad news is that it will turn your world inside out, as your identity and relationships will be forever changed.

But, thankfully, there's more good news. Ultimately, after a difficult transition, your world will be a more pleasant one to live in.

I recently had a caller who came on the air primed to paint her own portrait for me in just a few phrases: molested as a child, alcoholic stepfather, and a number of surgeries on her ankles. She listed all these with a halting voice and choked back tears.

"Do you think," she asked me, "that all or some of these could be the reason I'm depressed?"

Without answering, I asked her if she was married.

"Yes, to a wonderful and patient man."

I followed with a question about children.

"Yes, "she replied. "Two wonderful, beautiful children."

I asked her if she could walk.

"Yes, I'm lucky in that. Although the constant pain of these surgeries has been awful."

My next questions were, "Did your house blow away in a hurricane?" "Do you have cancer?" "Are any of your children suffering a fatal illness?"

And so on.

The answers to all these questions were no.

"Oh," I said.

She then went on to tell me that she hadn't told her husband about the sex play with her older sister until just about the time the surgeries were over. I thought that was very interesting.

"I wonder what you wanted to get from him at the time you told him."

She didn't answer.

"Was his sympathy for the ankle surgeries wearing off? Were you wanting sympathy?"

"Yes," she said quietly.

For this caller, keeping the bag of bad memories and experiences around her neck was her way of ensuring sympathy and caretaking and her version of love. It was as though her historical pains were small treats to keep people around her and caring for her.

Clearly, she didn't believe she could get that caring without maintaining the pain.

I often ask people in similar situations to think of the horrible memory and let the feeling wash over them. You can feel their agitation. I follow that up by suggesting that they now slip into visualizing something current that is wonderful, warm, safe, loving, fun.

You can feel their elevated mood. I have them go back and forth several times to reassure themselves that they indeed do have the power to create any mood at any moment.

The problem then becomes one of giving up the perks of feeling bad: the attention, concern, support, caring, and forgiveness for not being responsible.

This is definitely the part of the transition that is the most difficult. Telling somebody that people will love them for who they are doesn't work because they don't think they are worth love. However, telling somebody that people will love them for the love they give does work—but only when they are able to come out of their own fears and open their hearts to the needs and feelings of others.

DR. LAURA SAYS:

I wrote *Bad Childhood–Good Life* to help people make this admittedly difficult transition. It is usually more powerful to work with intimates while making these healthy changes, as your change requires them to change too.

Your Body Is Your Responsibility—So Get Fit!

"My genetics made me do it!" "My hormones made me do it!" "My self-esteem made me do it!" "My emotions made me do it." "Actually, I don't know what made me do it!" What's the "it"? The "it" is getting fat.

You would think that my positions on abortion, sex education in the public schools, day care, divorce, shacking up, single mothers by choice, and so forth, would be the biggest stimulants to angry mail. Nope. It is when I point out that fat is voluntary and an issue of laziness that the floodgates open. I remind people that being fat is about simple math: If you take in more calories than you expend, you will gain weight.

I remember one particular call from a husband and wife asking me to help them with their problem. It seems that the wife, in her twenties, has gained considerable weight since they married. Her husband mentioned to her that she looks good, but she'd be back to being "hot" if she took off that weight. She was calling to have me slam him for being hurtful and insensitive.

"Are you fatter than just a few years ago?" I asked her.

"Well, yes, I guess I am," came the sullen reply.

"So why are you mad at him for telling you the truth? I thought we women wanted men who communicated with us," I said.

"Well, he hurt my feelings," she sulked.

"Really? What a great way to avoid dealing with your responsibility here—turn it around on him so that he's the bad guy and you no longer have to expend the effort to improve your eating habits and exercise efforts. Very smart! My dear, you know what you have to do—instead of getting all defensive and hostile with your beloved husband over your extra fat, ask him to help you work it off and change your family's eating habits."

Her husband was only partially happy with the phone call; he still believed he was going to be punished and wondered aloud about ever commenting on anything like that again. I reminded them both that they had to get better at working together, not become hypersensitive and avoidant.

A study from the Sansum Diabetes Research Institute in Santa Barbara, California, demonstrates that the fat that runs in families is largely LEARNED and NOT genetic. The researchers found that fat mothers (average 187 pounds and 5 feet tall) gave their babies more food, allowed them to sleep longer, and played with them less than slimmer (126 pounds and 5 feet 2 inches tall) mothers. The same study also found that there were no significant differences in the energy expenditure of metabolic rates of the babies born to fat and normal weight mothers.

Studies also show that childhood obesity has quadrupled since the 1980s. Chubby kids tend to grow into oversized adults: Studies evidently show that between 70 percent and 80 percent of overweight teens grow into overweight adults. Habits are hard to break.

So while many people are suing fast-food restaurants for "making them fat," and others blame their hectic lifestyle that leaves them little time for shopping and preparing healthy meals, my perspective is that your lifestyle and your choice of foods are all voluntary. I notice all the time, especially at lunches, that the fat people are having cheeseburgers, French fries, chocolate cake, and so forth, while the thin people are having salads with the dressing on the side and fruit instead of potatoes.

I personally work too hard at staying trim and fit to tolerate the whining, blaming, and hostility of fat folks who don't want to put in the effort. I had a three-month period during which I ate half a bag of blue tortilla chips each day after work: Eight pounds appeared on that scale seemingly overnight! Now, not a blue chip makes it into my house; it is the only food I apparently have no control over. However, I will eat ONE cookie and feel quite content and have no guilt, which would drive me to overeat to make myself feel better. I can probably outeat most other adults even younger than me, but I keep to fish, chicken, big salads, fruit desserts (except at events), and few fried foods ever. I am 5 feet 3 inches tall and weigh 113 because I work at it!

I think our culture has drained away the notion of earning things. For example, instead of awards ceremonies for excellence hard earned, many schools are giving some kind of award to every student, so the students won't feel bad. Too many parents are paying for everything for their teen and young adult children, so they won't suffer from doing without.

DR. LAURA SAYS:

The more we cater to feelings and making things easy, the less our children will live up to the potential of the historical grit in which Americans prided themselves.

REFLECTIONS

Consider how often you do something you know darn well is wrong because you just don't want to deal with the short-term suffering that comes from abstaining.

This can include anything from smoking, eating, going back to an abusive spouse, dating or marrying one alcoholic after another, working desperately to make an unloving parent care about you, and on and on.

Here's the reality: You will probably have to endure time in pain as you accept the truth of your bad situation. Finally—finally!—you'll get it. It will be gut-wrenching—but only then will it be over. Freedom from a hopeless desire. From that point on, you will seek out relationships with people who will be there for you.

Without opening yourself to that needed suffering, you will spend your years on a gerbil wheel, never getting anywhere. Do you want to make the most you can out of your life? The hard truth is that the key to growth is suffering.

Stop avoiding it. Embrace the pain. It will set you free and put you on a path to peace and happiness.

CHAPTER FIFTEEN

Faith & Country

People would often say to me about my radio program, "What you say is common sense." Well, that might have been the case once, but it isn't so much anymore. Common values are lacking from our families, communities, and schools.

Fourth of July Sparks Hope for a Better Nation

In the first week of July, most of us get excited about the celebrations, fireworks, barbecues, and parades. There's a general sense of pride in being an American.

Sadly these days, too many folks are not feeling like there is much to celebrate as they watch the things they value become tainted.

This is how I felt when I heard about Christian Stanfield, a 15-year-old boy whose story has mostly flown under the national media radar. Christian—diagnosed with comprehension delay, anxiety disorders, and ADHD—was the victim of bullying by fellow students in his special education math class at South Fayette High School in McDonald, Pennsylvania. He has a low processing speed, and some people get frustrated by that—frustrated enough evidently to torment him.

In an attempt to get help, Christian used his iPad to record his harassers. It didn't work. Those doing the bullying were not disciplined. Instead, the school principal and superintendent contacted police because they thought Christian had violated wiretapping laws. Indeed, he was cited and convicted of disorderly conduct for making the recording.

Christian explained why he made the tape, which documented bullies making vulgar comments about him: "I wanted some help. This wasn't just a one-time thing. This always happens every day in that class."

I get why the school tried to hide its lack of protection of bullied students. I don't get why a court in the United States of America would punish him for making a record, getting proof of his tormentors so that someone would help him.

Thankfully, charges have been dropped. However, damage has been done. Christian has been traumatized tremendously, having lost weight, requiring therapy, missing school, and made to seem like the perp instead of the victim.

The topper is that this young man doesn't want revenge. His mother, Shea Love, is quoted as saying: "What I want is for heads to roll. But he said to me, 'Mom, it might make you feel better if people get fired, but that won't change anything.' He said there needs to be more compassion for people."

Police have cameras now to document all traffic stops. I assume that is to protect themselves from false accusations and have documented evidence for trials. A 15-year-old doesn't have the same right?

DR. LAURA SAYS:

On any Fourth of July, I hope we can all find a reason to feel proud of our great nation and figure out a way to make it better in the future—especially for good people like Christian Stanfield.

Beliefs and Traditions

It is always sad and frustrating for me to see how many people rooted deeply in moral beliefs and traditions will dump them at a moment's notice for fear that someone will be displeased with them.

It is also thrilling for me to see some of those people rise to the occasion, honor their beliefs with courage, and confront criticism and risk rejection.

Lynette started out as the former and ended up as the latter. A justice of the peace, she called me for advice about whether or not she should perform a wedding service for one of a group of seven women friends who met weekly. Everyone had gotten into celebratory gear and began volunteering to do things for the wedding and shower: cakes, flowers, ring pillows, garter, etc. They then turned to Lynette and asked her to perform the wedding. She agreed. That was before she heard the rest of the story.

She found out that the groom-to-be was 36 (her friend is 27), has three illegitimate children by two women, and was not allowed to take the children from their mothers' homes for visits (Lynette never knew why, and her "friend" didn't seem to consider any of that important). Her friend and the guy had been living together in her friend's mother's basement for two years, and they were trying to have a baby!

Lynette knew this was wrong and yet struggled with the pull to stay part of this social group as opposed to standing up for her morals and values. This is when she called me. She knew it was wrong for her to officiate, but she was scared to confront these women and pronounce her values so blatantly. She only had a few days until the next dinner gathering.

Frankly, I let her have it . . . lovingly, of course. What is the point of having morals, ethics, and values when one doesn't back them up with the hard choices that give testimony to their value? If they can be dumped for something as small as not getting criticized, they can't be very important in the first place. Furthermore, I said, if you let this go and participate in this service, aren't you supporting several levels of cruelty to children? I told her she had a moral obligation to her friend to reject these behaviors.

Lynette wavered, but emailed me that she told the women this:

> We have all forgotten our moral obligations here, thinking only of trying to please and remain friends. It is after careful consideration, and moral debate, that I have come to the conclusion that it is in the best interest of Keith's three children that I do not perform the marriage ceremony. I cannot and will not condone it. Children come first, and should be given the attention of both parents. Parents with minor children should not remarry until the youngest is 18 and out of the house. [For this man] to marry and take that attention he devotes to her away from his children is unconscionable and will have long lasting effect on the children. Children are the most important and most forgotten in circumstances such as this. To further state that they want to bring another child into this situation is even more unconscionable and selfish. It is appalling to think that grown, mature people who espouse high moral values would encourage and support this type of relationship. We should all be ashamed of ourselves!

I thought it was fabulous . . . but none of the women did. The only comment she got back was, "You should not have spoiled everything. The wedding is going to take place anyway and there is nothing you can do."

Well, Lynette did a lot; not perhaps to stop this travesty, but to be courageously public about value and responsibility to others. The other women may be too weak to heed her words, but there are five lessons in those words for us all:

1. Being liked is not being respected; respect is more important.
2. Making judgments on right and wrong is necessary
3. Standing up for your beliefs can bring rejection and ridicule. Be proud—those are defensive reactions.
4. Write down and practice your words, if you need to speak your position clearly.
5. Be patient: It takes time for a seed to germinate. The first response isn't always the last.

DR. LAURA SAYS:

It takes guts to stand up in public for your values and responsibilities toward others. But it's always the right thing to do.

Public Schools Have Become Enemies of Freedom

One morning I came across two stories that seemingly had nothing whatsoever to do with each other, though I could see the link as clear as day and as scary as zombie movies.

The first story's headline: "Pa. Bishop Does Not Recant Saying That Hitler and Mussolini 'Would Love Our Public School System.'" According to *CNS News*, Bishop Joseph McFadden made a comparison between the interests of the public school system and totalitarianism, while discussing what he saw as a lack of school choice in Pennsylvania.

"The reference to dictators and totalitarian governments of the 20th century which I made in an interview on the topic of school choice [aka 'vouchers'] was to make a dramatic illustration of how these unchecked monolithic governments of the past used schools to curtail the primary responsibility of the parent in the education of their children," he said.

The headline of the second story, from the *Telegraph* in Great Britain, read: "Girls, 13, Given Contraceptive Implants at School." The story went on to say, "Girls as young as 13 have been fitted with contraceptive implants at school without their parents knowing." The *Telegraph* noted that it was part of a government—government—initiative to drive down teenage pregnancies.

As many as nine secondary schools in the city of Southampton were thought to be involved. The health chiefs had defended this, saying teenage pregnancies had dropped by 22 percent. They didn't, however, tell us how much promiscuity and STDs have risen as boys tell girls to get the implant so they can have sex without mum and dad being the wiser. And they didn't tell us how much these youngsters would be emotionally and psychologically damaged by reckless so-called safe-sex behaviors.

As one parent said, "Parents send their children to school to receive a good education, not to be undermined by health workers who give their children contraceptives behind their backs."

The ADL and the ACLU don't see the reason Bishop McFadden made reference to totalitarian governments? Are the ADL and ACLU skirting the real issue by being "offended" that there is a connection between totalitarian governments and mass murder: Syria, Libya, Egypt, Iran, Soviet Union, Northern Korea, Cambodia, etc.? Shall I go on?

Many schools across the country invite Planned Parenthood representatives to their schools to give "information" on "family planning." (I call it recruitment of future abortions.)

In America, our public schools will teach about every sexual combination and orientation of existing sexual experience as morally equal and acceptable, disallowing discussion, much less disagreement.

DR. LAURA SAYS:

This is pretty standard for public schools and is why I always recommend that children be taken out of public schools and put in conservative religious schools or be homeschooled. Our public schools have become politically correct sites of manipulation of thought and beliefs. The bishop was right.

REFLECTIONS

Parents have to be aware, be informed, and stand up for the values they hold dear. If it means you "fight the system," homeschool, or choose private religious school—make it happen. There are far too many children who need protection from activists' social engineering desires. Focus on instruction in history (unredacted), math, science, art, and so forth, which they will need in order to be informed citizens.

Afterword

96 Kinds of People Who Hate Dr. Laura (and Dr. Laura Loves It!)

I thought my readers would get a kick out of a post by Ken Paris, who has a blog called Everything Must Go! His blog name is "tuna safe dolphin," and you can read more at https://tinyurl .com/y5r6gmwd. This post is reprinted with his permission.

Dr. Laura has angered off a lot of people. Here's a list that I do not claim to be exhaustive.

In no particular order:

1. Fat people. That's about 2/3rds of Americans. More precisely, she's enraged the ones who don't like to be told they can and should do something about it, but that solution is not some magic pill.
2. People who like to imagine they are engaged even though there's no ring and no date.
3. Women willing to be easy, casual hook-ups and shack-ups. Schlessinger rains on their parade by telling them they don't have rights over the males with whom they are

having sex (nor do the males have any rights over them) and that they are making life harder for decent women.

4. Men who don't want women like the ones described above wising up about sex.

5. Women who insist on a large, traditional wedding, especially with a white dress, and all of the traditional trappings and parties that have been added over the years, many of whom demand their parents pay for it—after shacking up for years and even making babies. (More generally, people who want their parents to keep financially supporting them even as they flagrantly violate tradition, morality, or parental sensitivities.)

6. Parents who have chosen to raise their children in America but still want their children beholden to foreign traditions.

7. People who want to take their young children to weddings despite a lack of invitation.

8. Feminists, and guys who don't want to take responsibility for anything, but rather hide behind deference to feminism.

9. Men who don't want there to be an expectation that men always pay for everything on every date other than her cooking at home for him.

10. Men who want to date even though they can't yet afford to support a wife and kids.

11. Wives who want to withhold sex from their good husbands.

12. Parents who want to keep their adult children dependent in perpetuity or do not evict the 18 year-old or older offspring out of the home.

13. People who think having their own potential child or grandchild aborted is (or was) preferable to giving that child up for adoption or raising the child themselves.

14. People who make money off of abortions.

15. People who are in no position to provide a baby with a stable, married, mom-and-dad home who refuse to put the baby up for adoption.

16. Men who want to do something with the newly discovered information that they have been raising what turns out to be, biologically, another man's child.

17. Anyone else who thinks it is important to tell children their father is not their biological father or that there is some long-lost half-sibling out there somewhere.

18. Women who have learned their husband has another child who needs a father and don't want him to have any contact with that child.

19. People who think open adoption is better than closed adoption.

20. Adoptees raised by decent families who seek out their biological parents/siblings, especially with "medical history" as the excuse.

21. People who want to be surrogate wombs, or egg or sperm donors for a family member or friend.

22. Organ donation advocates who encourage the practice of living children donating to parents.

23. Women who don't want to raise their own children or have made choices that make it much more likely their children will be raised by strangers. Guys who want their wives to stick the children in day orphanages so their wives can earn income.

24. Day orphanage operators and other business owners who depend on the above women and guys.

25. People who want to intentionally raise a child without a mother or without a father, and "rights" groups that claim to represent them.

26. Divorced or never-married parents of minor children who want to date, (re)marry, and even make more children to the detriment of the children they already have.

27. Parents who drug their kids, especially boys, in response to normal behavior or normal reaction to the bad situation created by the parent(s).

28. People who make money off of such drugging.

29. So-called "children's rights" advocates who think that minors living at home should not be drug tested or have their diaries, communication devices, possessions, or rooms searched against their will.

30. Pedophiles and anyone who wants to have sex with your minor children.

31. People who think quick, light swats on the tush are child abuse.

32. Parents who want to be their child's buddy.

33. People who want to place their parents before their spouse.

34. People who want to come between spouses.

35. Adult children of widows or widowers who don't want their parent dating (yet).

36. People who want power over their stepchildren.

37. People jealous of their spouse's deceased previous spouse.

38. Adults who leave children alone in hot automobiles.

39. The authorities who neglect to prosecute such people.

40. Parents who demand that all of their children simultaneously ace all advanced placement classes, letter in at least two sports, and master a musical instrument, even if they hate those sports and hate playing music.

41. People who want their kids to excel in gymnastics or football.

42. People who think gay or lesbian people shouldn't be treated with respect, and if they weren't treated with respect, they'd all become happy heterosexuals.

43. Pacifists.

44. Adults who enjoy video games to excess.

45. People who hate dogs or, at least, hate hearing about them.

46. People who make or watch trashy so-called reality television.

47. People who want to complain to their deployed military spouses over and over again about something that deployed person can't address.

48. People who want to hurt their spouse or alleviate their guilt telling their spouse of an adulterous fling or affair that ended.

49. Adults who were victims of childhood sexual abuse who still haven't taken any steps to protect anyone else from the abuser.

50. Any adult who knew the abuse was going on, but did nothing about it.

51. Teacher union bosses who think they should be in control of how children are raised.

52. Guys who admit to women they date that they watch porn.

53. People who think married people should never watch porn.

54. Women who like to think they have a magic vagina that can change a man.

55. People who don't want to disclose to a potential employer that they have a disability, medical condition, or pregnancy.

56. People who think it is a great thing that the Americans With Disabilities Act prevents businesses from charging people to accommodate their service animals.

57. People who like to blame every lousy thing they or a loved one does on diseases or addictions.

58. People who want to raise children in "interfaithless" homes.

59. Therapists who like the steady income provided by clients coming to them to whine about the same things for years and years, and the people who like doing the whining.

60. Callers who want to go on and on whining, and the listeners who want to hear the whining.

61. People who hate Jews.

62. People who think practicing their "new" personal faith is more important than maintaining family unity by continuing to practice, and raise their children in, their "old" faith.

63. People who think that sex, porn viewing, eating, gambling, or shopping can be addictions.

64. People who think addiction is a disease.

65. Parents who think it is acceptable for kids to have their own phones and tablets, and the kids who want them.

66. People who think they or their kids should have a Facebook account (even though she invites people to comment on her show's Facebook page).

67. Anyone who thinks an agreement or promise between shack-up lovers matters, since they haven't taken marital vows in a legal marriage.

68. Anyone who thinks their marital vows still matter if there are no minor children and the other spouse has broken the vows, abuses substances or them, is more than ten years older or younger, has a significant incompatibility, or has some other red flag or serious character flaw.

69. Anyone who wants a prenup or any separate financial accounts for a first marriage.

70. Anyone who thinks it is OK for one spouse to have any passwords the other spouse doesn't know.

71. Anyone who thinks it would be beneficial to their child to have a sibling.

72. Cousins who have sex or marry (cousin marriage is legal in about half of the states).

73. Anyone who uses online matchmaking or dating services or apps.

74. Anyone who wants any form of mutually agreed-to non-monogamy or proposes in-person observation of other people having sex.

75. Vegetarians who want to raise their children as vegetarians.

76. Parents who want to require their children to eat specific kinds of meat.

77. Anyone who thinks being shy or introverted is OK.

78. People who believe anything in their life, especially healing from an ailment, is an actual miracle, or that a Supreme Being intervenes in life.

79. People who believe in soulmates.

80. People who believe there are guardian angels or that deceased friend or family member has any involvement in their life now.

81. (Young Earth) Creationists.

82. People who think bisexuals, bicurious, and heteroflexible people exist. (Any sex-like behavior with or attraction to someone of the same sex = gay.)

83. People who think midlife crises exist.

84. Guys who don't like it when someone, especially a woman, talks about what behavior makes a man a "real man."

85. Women or teen girls who want to call sex they later regret, or don't want to admit to their parents as having been sexually active, or mutually drunken sex "rape"; women or teen girls who have been raped but refuse to take responsibility for any bad decisions that left them vulnerable with a rapist (and their advocates).

86. Anyone who thinks it is acceptable for someone other than the married spouses to touch the marriage bed, even if it is just their child who wants comforting.

87. People who insist breastfeeding should be done in any public place without any covering or blanket.

88. Anyone who loves or defends pitbulls and mistakenly thinks Dr. Laura has said something against them (she said there were a bunch in a shelter that weren't going to be adopted and she said they should be put down because they were taking up space in the shelter that other dogs, which will be adopted, could have).

89. Anyone who identifies as a "cancer survivor" or "cancer warrior" in a way that implies they beat cancer by their own efforts as though people who were killed by cancer didn't try or weren't good enough at fighting it; anyone who credits their survival to anything but medical treatment and luck.

90. People who want to buy automobiles for their children/ grandchildren/nieces/nephews, especially if they are minors.

91. People who refuse to vaccinate their children at all (unless they know for sure the child will be harmed by the vaccine), especially if they don't want other people vaccinating their children.

92. People who think nobody should get a tattoo.

93. People who don't think phrases like "limp d---" or words like "s---" should be used by a satellite radio host/podcaster.

94. Any woman who has been sexually harassed or assaulted, especially in a professional setting, who kept quiet about it rather than doing anything legally possible to expose and stop the abuser.

95. Anyone who thinks it is a good idea for someone to do a DNA-genealogy/ancestry test or to make or accept contact based on such tests, and anyone selling such services (see 16, 17, 19, 20).

96. Anyone who thinks pranks can be fun instead of sadistic.

Is there anybody left???

Index

About Dr. Laura

As one of the most popular talk show hosts in radio history, **Dr. Laura Schlessinger** offers no-nonsense advice infused with a strong sense of ethics, accountability, and personal responsibility; she's been doing it successfully for more than 40 years, reaching millions of listeners weekly. Her internationally syndicated radio program has been heard exclusively on SiriusXM since 2011 (currently on Triumph Channel 111) and is also available via streaming, download, and podcast.

She's the author of 13 *New York Times* best sellers and four children's books, her books ranging from the provocative (for adults, *The Proper Care & Feeding of Husbands)* to the poignant (for children, *Why Do You Love Me?*). Her support of children and family values is legendary, and she is, indeed, "her kid's mom." She's on Facebook (facebook.com/drlaura), Instagram (instagram.com/drlauraprogram), Twitter (@drlauraprogram), and Pinterest (pinterest.com/drlaura), where she interacts daily with listeners. She has raised millions of dollars for veterans and their families, donating the proceeds from sales in her online boutique, at DrLauraDesigns.com, where she sells silver jewelry and glass art that she designs and creates. Proceeds from the sales in her boutique currently benefit the charitable Children of Fallen Patriots Foundation. She also writes a monthly column for *Newsmax Magazine.*

Dr. Laura holds a Ph.D. in physiology from Columbia University's College of Physicians and Surgeons, and she received her postdoctoral certification in marriage, family, and child counseling from the University of Southern California. She was in private practice for 12 years. She's also been on the faculty of the Department of Biology at the University of Southern California and a member of faculty of the Graduate Psychology Department at Pepperdine University.

She is one of the few civilians granted an award from the Office of the Secretary of Defense for her Exceptional Public Service. In 2018, she was named to the National Radio Hall of Fame. She received the Genii Award from the American Women in Radio and Television and the Chairman's Award from the National Religious Broadcasters, was named Woman of the Year by the Clare Boothe Luce Policy Institute, and was the first woman to win the National Association of Broadcasters' prestigious Marconi Award for Network/Syndicated Personality.

As skipper, Dr. Laura has won dozens of trophies in sailboat races and regattas and competed in the 2001 Transpacific Yacht Race ("Transpac") from California to Hawaii. She is also a black belt in martial arts.

Visit Dr. Laura: www.drlaura.com.

Books by Dr. Laura Schlessinger

Surviving a Shark Attack on Land: Overcoming Betrayal and Dealing with Revenge (2011)

In Praise of Stay-at-Home Moms (2009)

Stop Whining, Start Living (2008)

Bad Childhood–Good Life: How to Blossom and Thrive in Spite of an Unhappy Childhood (2007)

The Proper Care & Feeding of Marriages (2007)

The Proper Care & Feeding of Husbands (2006)

The Ten Commandments: The Significance of God's Laws in Everyday Life (2005)

Woman Power: Transform Your Man, Your Marriage, Your Life (2004)

Ten Stupid Things Couples Do to Mess Up Their Relationships (2002)

Ten Stupid Things Men Do to Mess Up Their Lives (2002)

Ten Stupid Things Women Do to Mess Up Their Lives (2002)

Stupid Things Parents Do to Mess Up Their Kids: Don't Have Them if You Won't Raise Them (2001)

How Could You Do That?! The Abdication of Character, Courage, and Conscience (1996)

STAY IN TOUCH WITH
DR. LAURA SCHLESSINGER

Listen on SiriusXM
Triumph 111
Monday-Friday 2-5pm Eastern

TRI☼MPH

Stay connected with
Dr. Laura's Call of the Day Podcast available at
Apple Podcasts, Pandora, Spotify, and Stitcher

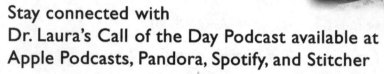 CALL OF THE DAY

Subscribe to the Dr. Laura Premium Family Podcast
Listen anytime, anywhere on any device!
Subscribe at DrLaura.com

Join the Dr. Laura Family - DrLaura.com
Follow her on Facebook and Instagram
Facebook.com/DrLaura and @DrLauraProgram
Take her video course at Marriage101.com

NOW GO DO THE RIGHT THING!

Dr Laura

More Titles From Humanix Books You May Be Interested In:

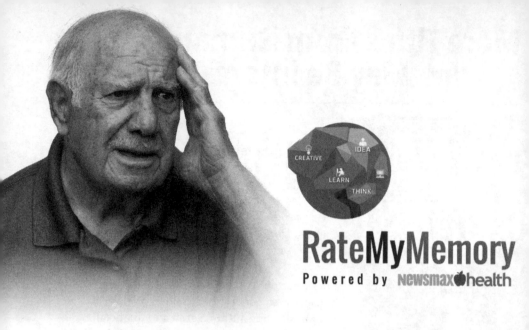

Simple **Heart Test**

Powered by Newsmaxhealth.com

FACT:

▶ Nearly half of those who die from heart attacks each year never showed prior symptoms of heart disease.

▶ If you suffer cardiac arrest outside of a hospital, you have just a 7% chance of survival.

Don't be caught off guard. Know your risk now.

TAKE THE TEST NOW ...

Renowned cardiologist **Dr. Chauncey Crandall** has partnered with **Newsmaxhealth.com** to create a simple, easy-to-complete, online test that will help you understand your heart attack risk factors. Dr. Crandall is the author of the #1 best-seller *The Simple Heart Cure: The 90-Day Program to Stop and Reverse Heart Disease.*

Take Dr. Crandall's Simple Heart Test — it takes just 2 minutes or less to complete — it could save your life!

Discover your risk now.

- **Where you score on our unique heart disease risk scale**
- **Which of your lifestyle habits really protect your heart**
- **The true role your height and weight play in heart attack risk**
- Little-known conditions that impact heart health
- **Plus much more!**

SimpleHeartTest.com/Love